The
Childhood of Religions

(1878)

Embracing a Simple Account of the Birth
and Growth of Myths and Legends

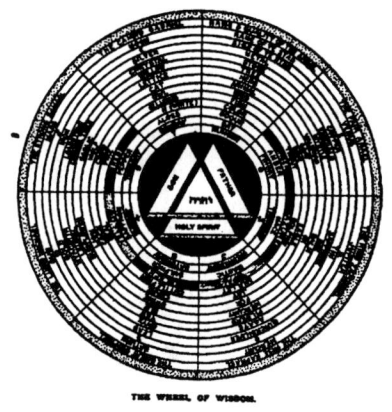

THE WHEEL OF WISDOM.

Edward Clodd

ISBN 0-7661-0502-4

Request our FREE CATALOG of over 1,000
Rare Esoteric Books
Unavailable Elsewhere

Freemasonry * Akashic * Alchemy * Alternative Health * Ancient Civilizations * Anthroposophy * Astral * Astrology * Astronomy * Aura * Bacon, Francis * Bible Study * Blavatsky * Boehme * Cabalah * Cartomancy * Chakras * Clairvoyance * Comparative Religions * Divination * Druids * Eastern Thought * Egyptology * Esoterism * Essenes * Etheric * Extrasensory Perception * Gnosis * Gnosticism * Golden Dawn * Great White Brotherhood * Hermetics * Kabalah * Karma * Knights Templar * Kundalini * Magic * Meditation * Mediumship * Mesmerism * Metaphysics * Mithraism * Mystery Schools * Mysticism * Mythology * Numerology * Occultism * Palmistry * Pantheism * Paracelsus * Parapsychology * Philosophy * Plotinus * Prosperity & Success * Psychokinesis * Psychology * Pyramids * Qabalah * Reincarnation * Rosicrucian * Sacred Geometry * Secret Rituals * Secret Societies * Spiritism * Symbolism * Tarot * Telepathy * Theosophy * Transcendentalism * Upanishads * Vedanta * Wisdom * Yoga * *Plus Much More!*

KESSINGER PUBLISHING, LLC

http://www.kessingerpub.com

email: books@kessingerpub.com

THE

CHILDHOOD OF RELIGIONS:

EMBRACING

A SIMPLE ACCOUNT

OF THE

BIRTH AND GROWTH OF MYTHS AND LEGENDS.

BY

EDWARD CLODD, F. R. A. S.,

AUTHOR OF
"THE CHILDHOOD OF THE WORLD."

"We were all brothers, because we had one work, and one hope,
and one All-Father."—*Alton Locke*, p. 273.

NEW YORK:
D. APPLETON AND COMPANY,
549 & 551 BROADWAY.
1878.

PREFACE.

IN a little book entitled 'The Childhood of the World,' which was received by the public with unlooked-for favour, an attempt was made to convey to young persons the knowledge concerning man's early condition which has been gathered during recent years, and it is to the Second Part of that work, which treats of his advance from lower to higher stages of religious belief, that the present volume, which deals mainly with the expression and embodiment of that belief in certain great religions of the East, is intended to be supplemental.

The question which forces itself upon all who are interested in the education of the young, is what they shall be taught regarding the relation of the Bible to other sacred scriptures, and to the declarations of modern science where they fail to harmonise with its statements; and it is as a humble contribution to the solution of that question, that the present and preceding volumes have been written.

In an age which has been truly characterised by a leading thinker as one of 'weak convictions,' it seems to me incumbent on those who, in accepting the conclusions to which the discoveries of our time point, regard the inevitable displacement of many beliefs without fear, because assured that the great verities remain, to be faithful to their convictions, and to show that the process of destruction is removing only the scaffolding which, once useful, now obscures the temple from our view.

In the absence of any like elementary treatise upon subjects regarding which much ignorance and apathy prevail, and the treatment of which is at present confined to works for the most part high-priced, and not always accessible, I hope that this book may not be regarded as needless, however far it falls short of the requirement which appears to me to exist, and which it ventures to temporarily supply.

The mass of material at one's disposal renders

its clear presentment within a moderate compass somewhat difficult, but I have been at pains to select the essential portions, and, in view of those to whom the body of the work is addressed, to choose the simplest language which the several subjects permit. If the style is thus more familiar than dignified, I hope it may with greater success attract the ear of the youthful reader.

The Notes which are placed at the end of the book may be found useful to parents and teachers, as well as to those who may hereafter desire to pursue the matters to which it is designed to serve as a simple introduction, while the references affixed will indicate some of the authorities to whom I am under obligation. The number of these prevents specific acknowledgment, but I cannnot omit expressing much indebtedness to Profs. Max Müller, Whitney, and De Gubernatis, and to Drs Muir, Tylor, Legge and the lamented Dr Deutsch, for the aid afforded by their works in the preparation of this book. The contributions of Professor Max Müller and Dr Muir to the subject of Comparative Theology are of the highest value to the student, while in all that relates to the development of mythology and religion among mankind the study of Dr Tylor's unsurpassed volumes on 'Primitive Culture' is indispensable.

E. C.

133, BRECKNOCK ROAD, LONDON,
March 1875.

CONTENTS.

CHAP.		PAGE
I.	INTRODUCTORY	1
II.	LEGENDS OF THE PAST ABOUT THE CREATION	10
III.	CREATION AS TOLD BY SCIENCE	29
IV.	LEGENDS OF THE PAST ABOUT MANKIND	43
V.	EARLY RACES OF MANKIND	53
VI.	THE ARYAN OR INDO-EUROPEAN NATIONS	67
	A. THE ARYANS IN THEIR UNDIVIDED STATE	70
	B. THEIR CIVILIZATION	75
	C. SOURCE OF OUR KNOWLEDGE ABOUT THEM	78
	D. THEIR RELIGION	86
	E. THEIR MYTHS	96
	F. THE SEPARATION OF THE ARYAN TRIBES	128
VII.	THE ANCIENT AND MODERN HINDU RELIGIONS	136
VIII.	THE ANCIENT RELIGION OF PERSIA	158
IX.	BUDDHISM	170
X.	THE RELIGIONS OF CHINA	189

CONTENTS.

		PAGE
XI.	THE SEMITIC NATIONS	200
XII.	MOHAMMADANISM, OR ISLAM	204
XIII.	ON THE STUDY OF THE BIBLE	230
	CONCLUSION	241

APPENDIX.

NOTE A.	*On the likeness between certain Chaldean and Jewish legends*	255
B.	*On the origin of the Solar System*	258
C.	*On the punishment of animals and lifeless objects as the cause of injury to Mankind*	259
D.	*On the supposed birthplace of Mankind*	260
E.	*On the common origin of Fairy Tales*	262
F.	*The sacred books of Hinduism*	264
G.	*On the words Brahmă or Brahm and Brahmâ*	270
H.	*The sacred books of the Pârsî religion*	271
I.	*Legends relating to the birth of Buddha*	273
K.	*The sacred books of Buddhism*	275
L.	*The sacred books, or Classics, of the Chinese*	277

INDEX 281

THE CHILDHOOD OF RELIGIONS.

CHAPTER I.

INTRODUCTORY.

A POET who has put many wise and tender thoughts into verses full of music, once wrote some lines on the birthday of a great and good man, whose life's delight was in listening to all that Nature has to tell, and who not long since passed away from earth to learn new lessons in some other part of the wide universe of God.

The poem tells us that as the boy lay in his cradle,

> 'Nature, the old nurse, took
> The child upon her knee,
> Saying: "Here is a story-book
> Thy Father has written for thee."
>
> ' "Come wander with me," she said,
> "Into regions yet untrod;
> And read what is still unread
> In the manuscripts of God."

'And he wandered away and away
  With Nature, the dear old nurse,
Who sang to him night and day
  The rhymes of the universe.

'And whenever the way seemed long,
  Or his heart began to fail,
She would sing a more wonderful song,
  Or tell a more marvellous tale.'

It is some fragment of the wonderful story 'without an end' to which Agassiz (for it is he of whom Longfellow speaks in the poem) listened so gladly, a story as true as it is wonderful and as beautiful as it is true, that I want to tell you, if you too wish to open your young eyes to the sights that ever grow more charmful, and your ears to the sounds that give forth no unsweet notes; otherwise the story is not for you.

To learn well the lessons which Nature is ever willing to teach, we must begin while we are young, for then the memory is 'wax to receive and marble to retain.' The mind, like a knife, quickly rusts if it be not used. Unless the eye is trained to see, it becomes dim; unless the ear is trained to hear, it gets dulled; and this is why so many, careless to sharpen their wits on the whetstone of outlook and thought, enter into life and pass away from it, never knowing in what a world of beauty, of bounty and of wonder they have lived.

So I would have you treasure the joy which earth and heaven yield as riches that no moth or rust can corrupt or thief break through and steal; that make the poorest boy who smiles his thanks for the bit of blue sky that roofs the murky court in which he lives, happier, and therefore wealthier, than the richest lord whose sunlit acres of woodland and meadow call from him nothing but a yawn.

I think you will be interested in listening to a few curious stories in which men of old have striven to account for the universe, how it all began to be and what keeps it going. Some of these stories have only come to light during the last few years, and this through the patient labours of learned scholars, who have found them buried in the sacred writings of certain religions of the East. We will then see what our men of science have learned from the story-book of Nature about the earth's history in the ages long, long ago, when as yet no man lived upon it;

when no children, with eyes laughter-filled, made nosegays of its flowers, and ran after the jewels which they were told lay sparkling where the rainbow touched the ground; but when God, ever-working, never-resting, since work and rest with Him are one, was fitting it to be the abode of life.

Following the same sure guides into that dim old past, we will learn a little of the mighty changes which, wrought by fire and water, have given to the earth's face its rugged, ragged outline, and also a little about the strange creatures that lived and struggled and died ages before God's highest creature, man, was placed here. Then after telling how the earliest races of men slowly covered large parts of the earth, the way will be clear for an account of the great parent-nation whose many children have spread themselves over nearly the whole of Europe, over large portions of Asia, and, since its discovery by Columbus, of America. We will learn something about the life these forefathers lived while together in one home, the language they spake, the thoughts that filled their breasts, and how those thoughts live on among us and other peoples in many shapes, both weird and winsome.

For I expect it will be news to some of you that the dear old tales which come now-a-days bound in green and gold and full of fine pictures, such as Cinderella, Snow-White and Rosy-Red, Beauty and the Beast, are older than any school-histories, and were told, of course in somewhat different form, by fathers and mothers to their children thousands of years ago in Asia, when Europe was covered with thick forests, amidst which huge wild beasts wandered.

I must stay here a moment to say that only a very little of what is now known concerning the matters already spoken of has been gathered from books. Men of science, wistful to learn more of that long before out of which we have come, have deemed none of its relics too trifling for their study. They have searched on the slopes of valleys through which rivers once flowed for the stone tools and weapons wherewith the first men worked and fought, and explored the caverns which from early times gave shelter to man and beast; they have opened great earth-mounds and tombs for remains of the dead laid within them; they have spelled out the picture-words painted on the walls of temples choked with the drifted sand of centuries, the wedge-shaped letters cut on rocks and stamped on sun-dried bricks, also the writing on crumbling papyri, dried palm-leaves, barks of trees and other substances; they have traced words in common use to the roots from which they sprang, and fairy tales and legends to the home of fancy where many of them were born; and thus has come to us, in ways undreamed of by our forefathers, rich treasures of knowledge.

Lastly, though by no means the least, we will open some of the sacred books of India, Persia, China, Arabia and other lands, to see for ourselves what the wisest and best of the ancients have thought about this wondrous life and what is to come after it. For *thought* rules the world. It makes no noise, but lives on and reigns when all the bustling and the shouting that seemed to stifle it are hushed, and whilst the great works which it guided the hand of man to do have perished, or remain to tell of pomp and glory gone for ever, it is with us in the words of wisdom that 'shall not pass away,' and to which we do well to give heed.

I have said how much life gains in *joyfulness* if our ears be kept open to the sweet voices of nature, and our eyes awake to its lovesome sights, and I would add how much it gains in *trustfulness* by even a slight knowledge of the religions which are at this day the hope and stay of hundreds of millions of our fellow-creatures. We learn therefrom how very near to his children the All-Father, to use the forceful name by which the old Norsemen called Him, has always been; near now, near in the days that are gone; and that there never was a time when He dwelt apart from men, caring not whether they were vile or holy, but that all age and place and human life is sacred with His presence. We shall learn, too,—

> 'That in all ages
> Every human heart is human;
> That in even savage bosoms
> There are longings, yearnings, strivings,
> For the good they comprehend not;
> That the feeble hands and helpless,
> Groping blindly in the darkness,
> Trust God's right hand in that darkness,
> And are lifted up and strengthened,'

so that when we read how poor wild souls, craving after the Power which they feel about them, are not able to rise above the worship of bunches of feathers or piles of stones, we shall know that it is the living God for whom they are feeling, and be sure that He will at last lead to Himself these children 'crying for a light.'

It gave men larger and grander views of God when they learnt that the earth is one among many bodies circling round the sun, and that the sun himself is one of numberless suns that are strewn as star-dust in the heavens, and it will give each of us, whose nature is made to trust, a larger trust in, and more loving thought of, Him to learn that our religion is one among many religions, and that nowhere is there an altogether godless race.

To use a homely figure, we shall see that the religions of the world are like human faces, all of which have something in common; nose, eyes, mouth, and so on; while all differ, some being more beautiful than others. And we shall also see that wherever any religion exists which has struck its roots deep down into the life of a people, there must be some truth in it which has nurtured them, and which is worth the seeking. For the hunger of the soul of man can no more be satisfied with a lie, than the hunger of his body can be appeased with stones. I am most wishful to impress this upon you, because you will never read the meaning of this world aright if you are content with that half-knowledge of the beliefs of other races, both savage and civilized, which most people have, and which suffices to give only false ideas of those beliefs.

Remember that where ignorance is, there is darkness; but that where knowledge dwells, light abides; and as knowledge of God, which comes from the study of man and his dwelling-place, the world, 'grows from more to more,' sunnier views of Him make glad the heart, chasing away the false ideas about Him that frightened poor timid, tender souls; that made even strong men shake, and bring their noble powers, tied and bound, before the grim Being they were taught to fear; that caused beauty to disfigure itself, as if ugliness was acceptable to Him, who 'hath made everything beautiful in its time.'

CHAPTER II.

LEGENDS OF THE PAST ABOUT THE CREATION.

IN every land and age man has looked up to the great, silent heaven, with its unresting sun, moon and stars; and upon this earth, with its robe of many folds and colours, and asked, 'Did these things make themselves? Had they a Maker? If so, how did He make them, and how long ago? What can He be like?' And the questions have had all kinds of answers framed to meet them, and not a few strange stories woven to explain the hard matter.

It is well known to you that among many beliefs, now found to be wrong, which were held in bygone days, people thought that the earth was a flat and fixed thing, for whose sole benefit the sun shone by day and the moon and stars by night. Now, such a belief as this is no matter for wonderment, because it was the only belief then possible. People must speak of things as they appear, and we still talk of the sun rising and setting, although we are sure he does nothing of the kind. If you had not learnt anything from books and other helps about the roundness of the earth and its movements in space, and had been shut up all your life in some wide plain where no hills broke the long, low line around, and gave you a sight, let us say, of the sea hiding in the distance the hulls of ships, you would have believed the earth to be flat and fixed, and lighted by the sun travelling daily across the sky, because your senses led you to such belief. Neither could you have learnt anything of the vastness and distance of the sun and stars, and you might have made the most simple guesses about these matters, as did some of the wise Greeks. One of them said that the moon was as large as that part of Greece once known as the Peloponnesus, but now called the Morea, and was laughed at for his boldness; while another held that the pale belt of light which is named, from a pretty myth, the Milky Way, and which we know consists of millions of stars, of which our sun is one, was the place where the two halves of the sky are joined together. And it was a very long time before people would believe that there were millions of mankind who were walking with their feet opposite to ours on another part of the earth.

But as the mind of man searched deeper into things many of them were found to be other than they seemed, and thus all truer knowledge as to what they are has been gained by slow and sure correction of that which the senses first told about them. It would fill a bigger book than this to tell through what paths of darkness and danger the master-spirits of old cut their way to light, amidst what silence and fear they worked, and with what trembling they told their discoveries to a trusted few, but the story is one you will do well to study. And now let us look at a few of the old legends about the beginning of things. They are for the most part but little known, and although the forms in which some of them are cast are crude and foolish, they are worth more than a smile. They were very real to those who framed them, and the wise will gladly find in them this truth : that in the presence of the great fact of earth, sea and sky, man has seen a greater fact than they, even a Cause without whom they had never been, a Cause to whom he has given many a different name and paid worship in many a strange fashion.

The spirit in which these early guesses at truth should be read is well enforced in this story, which comes from an ancient book added to one of the Vedas or sacred books of the Hindus.

A father tells his vain-minded son, in whom no sense of wonder dwells, to bring him a fruit of the huge banyan-tree or Indian fig-tree. 'Break it,' said the father; 'what do you see?' 'Some very small seeds,' replied the son. 'Break one of them; what do you see in it?' asked the father. 'Nothing, my father,' answered the son. 'My child,' said the father, 'where you see nothing there dwells a mighty banyan-tree.'

By way of comparing them with the stories which follow, it may be well to set down in simple outline the two accounts of the Creation which are given in the Book of Genesis.

In the *first account*, which is contained in chap. i. 1, to chap. ii. 3, we are told: 'In the beginning God created the heaven and the earth.'

On the *first* day light was created and divided from the darkness, thus causing day and night.

On the *second* day an expanse was formed above the earth, dividing the waters upon the earth from those which were to be stored as rain. (As Genesis vii. 11 shows, this expanse or dome was believed to be full of windows, which were opened whenever it was needful to let the rain through. The notion that the sky is a great roof covering in a flat world is an idea easily framed by the unlearned; the Polynesians, for example, call foreigners 'heaven-bursters,' as having broken in from another world outside.)

On the *third* day the remainder of the waters were gathered together as seas, and the land was made to bring forth grass and herb and tree.

On the *fourth* day God made two great lights, the sun and moon: 'He made the stars also.'

On the *fifth* day He peopled the waters with fishes and the dome above with birds.

On the *sixth* day the work of creation was ended by the earth bringing forth four-footed beasts and creeping things; man and woman, as the last and chiefest, being made 'in the image of God,' Who looked upon all that He had made, saw that it was good, and on the *seventh* day rested from His work.

The *second account*, which is given in Genesis ii. 4 to the end, speaks of the earth as without water and plants and trees, because there was no rain and not a man to till the ground.

Then the earth was watered by a mist, and man was made of the dust of the ground by the Lord God, Who breathed into his nostrils the breath of life so that he 'became a living soul.'

Man was then placed in the garden of Eden with leave to eat of the fruit of every tree except the tree of knowledge of good and evil. Then beasts and birds were made and brought to Adam that he might give them names. Last of all, the Lord God made a woman from a rib taken from Adam's side while he slept.

At this point you may ask, How are we to read these and other Bible stories? What they tell us about the creation, the early state of man, the universe in which we live, the age of the earth, and other kindred matters, differs so very much from what lesson-books on these subjects teach, that we feel puzzled which to believe.

The answer which I will try to give to this question before we pass on to the other legends may save you the irksome work of unlearning much in after years which is often taught upon these matters.

Since that which has to be said about one Bible legend applies to all the rest, we will deal with those already given about the Creation.

In bygone years people believed every word of those legends to be true, and there is a large number who still believe this, strangely overlooking the fact that the account given in the first chapter of Genesis of the mode and order in which things were made differs from the account given in the second chapter, and therefore that one of them must be wrong. After a time the Bible story seemed to be contradicted by the witness of those remains of the past which are found deep down in the earth, and although many books have been written with the view of showing that there is no real contradiction, each has failed to prove this. For this reason others have cast aside the narratives in Genesis as idle and meaningless tales which common sense and science alike bid us reject. From this you will see that *three* different views are held, upon each of which somewhat must be briefly said.

1. There are those who believe that God made all things in six days, that He fixed the sun and moon in the sky on the fourth day after the shedding forth of light and between the creation of plants and animals, because they find it thus written in the Bible.

Now it is not wise to accept anything as true *only* on the ground that we find it in a book, because if it turns out that the writer of the book was mistaken, that his knowledge is imperfect and his statements opposed to facts, the foundation upon which our belief rests is taken away and the belief goes with it. In reading books on history, science and any other subject, we believe that the writers have set down to the best of their knowledge all that can be said upon the matter, and we are glad to learn what they have to tell us, and, since very few have either time or talent to search for themselves, to rely thereon. But we are none the less ready, as are the writers themselves, to give up all if it is proved to be wrong, and to welcome the newer knowledge which the ages bring.

That we must apply this to the reading of the Bible I have sought to show at page 230. The unknown authors of Genesis, who it is thought compiled that book from older writings, and to whom the legends of other nations were known, as the likeness between the Jewish, Babylonian and Persian testifies, speak of the earth as made before the sun, and as arched over by a solid firmament. It was to them a flat thing that moved not, and since no voice has ever come from the unseen to instruct man in things which God has given him powers to find out, these writers were not wiser than the wisest of the age in which they lived. But the round earth was none the less moving in its course at the rate of nineteen miles in every second of time, else spring and summer, autumn and winter, had not then been.

If among the different sacred books of the world, for which, as will be seen hereafter, the same claims to be inspired every word are made by those who believe in them, there was one book quite free from mistakes and into which no blunder could by any means enter, we would gladly learn of it, since the truth-seeking can have but one desire, namely, to know what is true. But none such has ever existed, and never will exist, because every book is the work of man and therefore liable to error. That only is perfect which the finger of the Almighty has written on the rock-ribbed earth.

2. Those who hold that there is no real difference between the statements of the Bible and the facts of science, argue that when God is said to have made the heaven and earth in six days, it is not days of twenty-four hours each that are meant, but 'ages' or 'periods' of unknown yet vast duration.

We must all admit that it is very dangerous to force any meaning into words which, by unsettling what the user of them intended to convey, destroys their plain intent. They are far too sacred to have tricks played with them, and to give words more than one meaning is to make them mean whatever the fancy invents,

> 'For what the lips have lightly said,
> The heart will lightly hold.'

There can be no doubt that days are meant as such in Genesis, since to each day a 'morning' and an 'evening' is given (see chap. i., ver. 5, 8, 13, 19, 23, 31), and this, together with the fact that the appointment of the seventh day of the week as the Jewish Sabbath was based upon the hallowing of that day by God, proves that 'periods' and suchlike words which convey no idea of fixed lengths of time were not in the writer's mind.

The use of the number seven reminds us that certain numbers were accounted sacred by ancient nations, and that the old mystery about them still survives in foolish and unreasoning fears, and in proverbs as to the luck or ill-luck that attends them. The early worship of the sun, moon and five planets may explain the choice of seven as a sacred number among some eastern and western peoples, and so also may the apparent changes in the shape of the moon, known as her *phases*, which every seven days bring with them, and which account for the very early division of time into weeks.

This sacredness seems to have linked itself to the tradition of a creation in seven days and to the frequent use of that number in the Bible; these in their turn linking it to many legends of the Middle Ages, while the stories of seven sleepers, seven wise men, seven wonders of the world, and so on, also show what importance was given to it in olden times.

3. It is not wise or well to cast aside the Bible story. We can afford to be just to the past, and our debt to it is greater than we can pay, since its guesses made possible the sure knowledge of our time. However childish the ancient explanations of things may seem to us, they were the best that could be had. They were the work of honest men who, were they living now, would gladly correct their narratives by the great discoveries of these latter days. And those narratives contain for all time this truth, that every effect has a cause, and that this 'mighty sum of things for ever speak-

ing' witnesses to a Power able to produce and shape all to its own ends; a Power to which men give the name of GOD.

Therefore despise not the old because it is old, neither reject the new because it is new, but value each record of the past for the measure of truth which may be therein, since if it have none of that, it will perish, no matter how many millions believe it, nor with what shouts they strive to stifle the voices of those who believe it not.

Now we will pass on to other legends, beginning with the **Babylonian**,* the wild and ugly features of which are in strong contrast to the simpleness and quiet dignity of the story in Genesis. This legend, which is no doubt correctly given, comes to us through a Babylonian priest named Berosus, who lived in the time of Alexander the Great. The legend of the creation in the old Phœnician religion closely resembles it.

There was a time in which all was darkness and water. From these came hideous creatures; winged men, men with the legs and horns of goats;

* See Note A.

bulls with human heads, and suchlike monsters. Over all these was a woman, goddess of nature and mother of all beings, whom Belus, the chief of the gods, cut in two, making of one half the earth, and of the other half the sky. This caused the monsters to die, as they could not bear the light, upon seeing which Belus cut off his own head, and the gods then mixed the blood that flowed therefrom with the dust of the earth and formed man, which accounts for his sharing in the divine nature. Belus afterwards made the sun, moon, stars and five planets.

In the ancient religion of the Egyptians there is a legend that the sun wounded himself and that from the stream of his blood he created all beings.

Persian legend: from the sacred book of the Pârsîs, known as the Zend-Avesta. The Eternal Being produced two great gods, one named Ormuzd, King of Light, who remained true to him; the other named Ahriman, King of Darkness, who became the author of evil.

To destroy the evil, Ormuzd was appointed to create the world, which was made to last 12,000 years. He formed the firm vault of heaven and the earth on which it rests, and dwelt at the top of a mountain so high that it pierced the upper sky and reached the source of light. He then made sun, moon and stars to aid him in his battle with the terrible power of darkness; the universe being thus created in six periods; man, as in Genesis, last of all. The beautiful trust that dwelt in the heart of the pure-souled founder of the old Persian faith that good would in the end gain the victory over evil, will appear hereafter in the account of that religion.

Hindu legend: from an important book of the Brahman religion, called the Laws of Manu, the first part of which treats of Creation.

The universe was in darkness when Brahma (which means *force*), himself unseen, dispelled the gloom, first producing the waters and causing them to move. From a seed which he had placed in them there came a golden egg blazing with a thousand beams, and in this egg Brahma gave birth to himself. There he dwelt and at last split the egg in halves, one of which became the heaven and the other the earth.

(The Finns believed that heaven and earth were made out of a divided egg, the upper half being heaven, the yolk being earth, and the white fluid the all-surrounding ocean).

Brahma then drew forth mind and created a number of smaller gods and wise men, who in their turn created animals and demons, clouds, mountains and rivers.

You have doubtless heard of the Hindu notion that the earth rests upon animals standing one upon another, four elephants being placed lowest of all, because their legs *reach all the way down!*

Scandinavian legend:

> 'Once was the age
> When all was not,
> Nor sound nor sea
> Nor cooling wave.
> Nor earth there was
> Nor sky above,
> Nought save a void
> And yawning gulf,
> But verdure none.'

To the south of this yawning gulf there was a region of flame, and to the north an abode ice-cold and dark. Torrents of venom flowed from the north into the gulf and filled it with ice, but the fire came from the south, and, falling upon the ice, melted it. From the melted drops there arose the giant Ymir, who, wicked himself, had a wicked family of frost-giants. A cow was also formed from the melted ice, and she not only fed the giants with her milk, but out of the stones covered with salt and hoar-frost licked a man of strength and beauty, whose son became the father of Odin, Vili and Ve. These three slew Ymir, and out of his flesh they formed the earth; from his blood the seas and waters, from his bones the mountains, from his hair the trees, from his skull the heavens, from his brains the floating clouds, and from his eyebrows a wall round the earth to guard them from the giant sons of Ymir, whose anger they feared.

The old religion of the Scandinavians, who are a branch of the great German family, is contained in two books known as the 'Eddas,' a word thought to mean *Great-Grandmother* or *Ancestress*. The

Elder Edda contains the old mythic poems, and the Younger or Prose Edda such pagan legends as that just quoted, mixed with later ideas. Odin, the Alfadir, is therein thus spoken of:

'Gangleri began his speech: "Who is first or eldest of all gods?" Har said, "He hight Alfadir (is called All-Father) in our tongue, but in the old Asgard (or abode of the gods) he had twelve names."'

. . . 'Odin is named Alfadir because he is the father of all the gods, and also Valfadir (Choosing Father) because he chooses for his sons all who fall in combat, for whose abode he has prepared Valhalla' (Hall of the Chosen).

The old Norsemen spoke of death as *Heimgang:* that is, 'home-going,' a thought always beautiful and tender, but still more so as coming from these wild rovers of the 'homeless sea.'

Greek legend: from the Theogony, or 'Origin of the Gods,' said by some to be one of the works of Hesiod, an ancient poet. The Greek priests and wise men revered it greatly.

In the beginning there was huge and formless

Chaos, from whom came Gaia, the broad-bosomed earth, and Tartarus, dark and dim, below the earth. Then appeared beautiful Eros, or Love. From Chaos also came night and darkness, from these ether and day, whilst the earth gave birth to Uranus, the all-surrounding, starry heaven, and to the mountains and the sea. Then Gaia and Uranus married, and from them sprang demi-gods and men.

When you know more of the ancient peoples who worked out their thoughts about earth, sky and living things in such varied shape, and have learned amidst what different scenery each lived; how Frost and Fire had fierce unending battle, and the Ice-Giant his hearthless home where the hardy Norsemen dwelt; how sunshine and shadow made beautiful the well-wooded land of mountains and streams in the bright south where the Greeks dwelt; you will understand why one legend should impress us by its rugged grandeur and another enchant us with its stately grace.

CHAPTER III.

CREATION AS TOLD BY SCIENCE.

You have been taught that the earth is one of a number of *planets* (so called from a Greek word meaning *to wander*) which, with other bodies, travel round the sun, he being the centre of what is called the *solar* system (from Latin *sol*, the sun). Astronomy primers will tell you that every star is a sun, the centre of a solar system, and that our sun appears so large and bright because he is the star nearest to us.

It is believed that the particles of matter which compose the solar system (and what has now to be said applies to the formation of every other solar system) were once in a gas-like state, and in the vast space over which they were spread, so distant from one another as to be at rest. In the course of countless ages the immense mass became cooler through radiation, or loss of heat into space, and the particles were drawn closer together, and brought into a spinning motion, so that they became a huge self-shining, highly-heated mass, somewhat ball-shaped. The motion was quickened as the particles became more united, but when the force which swept them past the centre of the entire mass was greater than the force which dragged them towards it, rings of the outermost portion were thrown off one by one, which continued the wheel-like motion of the mass from which they had been cast. Each ring became broken at the points where the particles had clustered thickest, and these fragments, still spinning, gathered each round its centre, and threw off rings in like manner.

The huge ball in the centre of the whole became the *sun*, the ring fragments became the *planets* with their twofold motion, one top-like, the other round the sun, and the rings cast from them became their *moons*; each of these bodies being in a molten state. In the case of Saturn not only were eight moons formed, but there remain revolving round him the rings which so add to his beauty as an object in the telescope, and which are said to be made up of countless bodies.

The *comets* and streams of *meteors* which belong to our solar system were probably outlying fragments and smaller masses of the broken rings.*

Each body; sun, planet, moon, meteor, became globe-shaped in obedience to a law of the universe known as *attraction* (from Latin words meaning *drawn towards*). It is the law by which the dewdrop, the tear that falls from the eye, the melted lead dropped from the top of a tower where shot is made, become round. The little particles draw closely together, and in so doing arrange themselves around the centre, to which they are each *attracted*.

It is an important help to a clear understanding of the history of the earth to know what ground there is for the statement that each body of the solar system was in a molten condition.

Now there are certain forces in nature, such as light, heat, electricity, &c., each of which can produce, or be produced by, the rest. From this it has been concluded that they are different forms or modes of *one* unknown force that cannot be destroyed.

* See Note B.

Thus, to borrow an illustration of what is meant: In the case of a church spire struck by lightning, the force leapt from the cloud to the spire-cross as *light*; ran down the metal as *electricity*; melted it as *heat*; then burrowed through the stone-work till it got to metal again, splitting the stone in its course as *motion*; found the metal and ran harmlessly down it as *electricity*, but changing in its course probably the positions one to another of the atoms composing the metal, as *magnetism*; and then burst through the stone-work again as *motion*, so injuring the spire throughout that it had to be pulled down and re-built.

Therefore heat is not a substance, a subtle fluid, as was once thought, but a motion among the particles of matter. Bodies do not become heavier when they are heated, but they expand; that is, the heat drives their particles asunder, so that the minute spaces between them are widened and the body takes up more room. Knowing this, a smith, before he puts hoops on casks or tires round wheels, makes them red-hot. The heat expands them, and as they cool they shrink and bind tightly round the cask or wheel. And you know that two pieces of dry wood can be set on fire by being rubbed together, and that two pieces of ice can be melted in the same way, proving that heat is a 'mode of motion.'

The enormous *heat* of each body in the solar system was produced by the particles striking against one another as they were driven together by the force of *attraction*.

Another proof that the earth was once so hot as to be in a soft or melted state is afforded by its shape. It is not perfectly round, but slightly flattened at each pole, which was caused by its having been a fluid mass, spinning round like a top. In illustration of this, a lump of very soft clay or a mass of oil floating in liquid of the same density (or like weight bulk for bulk), will, when turned round, become flattened like the earth.

Again, the rocks forming part of the solid outside covering of the earth known as the *crust*, which have been fused together by fire, prove that the most intense heat must once have prevailed.

Every hot body which ceases to receive heat becomes cold; that is, parts with its heat; the larger the body, the longer it takes to cool, the outside cooling before the centre. The sun is so vast a body that he is still white hot, giving out heat, light and other forces. The moons being the smallest bodies were the first to cool; then the smaller planets, until we come to huge Jupiter and Saturn, which for aught we know may still be shedding some light and heat upon their moons. As each planet was once a small sun, there was a time, not to be counted by years, when the earth gave forth light and heat, and perchance supported life upon the now airless, sea-less moon.

And although the earth's crust had become cool and hard enormous ages back, there is still a vast store of heat below, which shows its power in the volcano belching forth its streams of lava; in the earthquake shaking down large cities and burying people in their ruins; and in the hot springs from which, chiefly in Iceland, jets of boiling water are thrown to a great height. The deepest mines, which, compared to the thickness of the earth, are but as scratchings on a school globe, are so hot that were it not for currents of fresh air the miners could not work in them. This store of heat is slowly but surely slipping away into space, so that finally the earth will become cold to its very core.

In brief, what the sun is the earth was millions of years ago; and what the moon now is the earth will be millions of years hence, when the flowers will bloom and the children romp elsewhere.

When the earth was a molten ball there were zones of vapour round it, which slowly condensed and fell as water into the valleys and cracks and lower levels of the cooling crust, filling them and thereby forming river, sea and ocean.

Of the mode in which, as the cooling went on, there fell from these zones different materials which helped to prepare the earth for the support of the life that was to appear thereon, or of the views held about the thickness of the crust and the nature of the matter beneath it, I cannot here speak. These are among the guesses of the wise, which may or may not be true, and we have already more of well-proved statement than this chapter can contain.

The crust of the earth is made up of rocks of many kinds and ages, all of which have been either laid down by water or melted and mixed together by fire. Of the former, some are composed of grains of various stones, and others largely or wholly of the remains of once-living animals and plants: the fire-fused rocks containing no traces of such remains. It is this crust which tells so surely the story of those vast changes of which the earth has been the scene, and which are still going on; how the heat within is rending the surface in one place and upheaving or sinking it in other places; how every little stream and brooklet is doing its work in altering the face of things, carrying soil to the sea, which is with hungry maw eating away the rock-bound coasts and softer fringes of the land; how, as the result of this, new continents and islands are slowly uprising from the ocean, to be one day dowered with the richest gifts of nature, studded with homesteads and cities, and the birth-place of wonders undreamt of which the spirit of man shall reveal; when the ocean will in its turn cover the happy homes of now the sunniest lands. All this is beyond question, for there is no rest in nature, not even in the things which look dullest and deadest; the particles that make up a stone being most likely ever moving, as we known the particles of a magnet are.

Professor Huxley, in describing the surprising movements of little bodies which course through the fluid in the hairs of the common stinging-nettle, just as like little bodies float in our blood, repairing the ceaseless waste of our frames, says that if our ears could catch the murmur of the currents whirling in the numberless cells which make up every tree, 'we should be stunned as with the roar of a great city.'

By way of illustration that the earth's face is ever changing, a study of its crust and a survey of its sea-depths tell us that our own island has been more than once buried under the waters. Since man first appeared, the greater part of the British Isles, of central Europe, of North America, and of northern Asia, have been beneath the sea, and the Caspian and Aral seas united as one great ocean. There is a legend of a lost island named Atlantis, placed by Plato west of the Pillars of Hercules in the Atlantic Ocean, and we know that the Canary Isles and the Azores are the highest peaks of the continent which lies beneath those waters. A name has already been given to a vanished land which once stretched from the eastern coast of Africa. Of this land, which there is good reason for thinking was the birthplace of mankind, Madagascar, Ceylon and other islands to the north-east, perhaps far into the Pacific Ocean, are the unburied parts. The great desert of Sahara was once covered by a sea whose waves dashed against the mountain ranges of northern Africa, and we shall learn further on that there was a time when those ranges were united to Europe.

No one knows how long a time passed between the molten state of the earth and the appearance upon its surface of the first forms of plant and animal life. That untold millions of years rolled away before the crust was cool enough to allow the steamy vapours above it to fall as water, is certain, and even then ages may have passed before other than the minutest kinds of life began to be. All that men of science can do is to get a rough idea of the time which it has taken to form à given thickness of certain layers of rock, each of which is called a *stratum* (from a Latin word meaning *spread out*).

For example: a very large portion of the earth's crust consists of chalk, which is made up of the shells of exceedingly small creatures that live and die under water, creatures of a kind that are at this moment forming chalk beds at the bottom of our oceans. A layer of chalk one foot thick is not heaped up in less than one hundred years and it probably takes a much longer time, so that, as the chalk beds in some parts of England exceed one thousand feet in thickness, we are on the safe side in reckoning that their formation occupied not less than one hundred thousand years. And as any table of the earth's crust will show you, there are rocks above and below the chalk, for the production of which millions heaped upon millions of years are required.

Such vast lengths of time may startle us to whom but a few years of life here are given, but they count not with Him Who is from everlasting to everlasting, and Who, working through the ages, has caused this earth to yield us that rich variety which 'age cannot wither.' And that variety too out of few materials; for the bodies we dwell in; the air we breathe; the water we drink; and every animal, tree and flower, are for the larger part formed of three gases, known to us as oxygen, hydrogen and nitrogen, each of which by itself is invisible, tasteless and without smell! Oxygen forms three-fourths of the uppermost crust of the earth.

In reading these names and the names given to other things, always seek the reason why they have been chosen, but at the same time remember that we know nothing as to what things are *in themselves*, and this will save you from many a boastful blunder of thinking that you know all about a substance because you have learnt its name. But in speaking of the few materials out of which such variety has come, there is something more wonderful to be said, and with it I must close this chapter.

It is, I hope, made clear to you, that the sun and all the bodies in his system are composed of the same materials, and by means of an instrument called a *spectroscope*, which enables astronomers to examine the light from the stars, no matter how many years it has been travelling to the earth, they are able to tell what metals are burning in those far-off bodies, and they find that those materials which are most plentiful in the stars are those which enter so largely into the structure of living creatures on the earth.

It is therefore no blind guess, but well-proved truth, that matter throughout the universe of God is the same in kind, but in different states. In the sun and his fellow-suns, the stars, it is white-hot; on the earth and some other planets (Mars, for example, on which a good telescope clearly shows the division of land and water and the increase of snow at the poles as the winter nears) it is cool enough to sustain life; in the moon and meteors it is cold and barren; while in some of the cloud-like clusters in the sky called *nebulæ* (from Latin *nebula*, a cloud), it is in a gas-like state.

Having said thus much, it would be needful to say a good deal more, but I am only acting as a finger-post to point what I think is the right road in which sound knowledge about this world's history can be gained. You need not think that the lesson will be quickly learned, or that the knowledge will ever be completed here. Science can never tell us all that we should like to know, or lead us beyond the veil 'where men grow blind though angels know the rest.' But we shall agree that her 'marvellous tale' has as much poetry in it as the old legends quoted, and certainly more of fact. The cloud-like mass becomes a cooled globe, a fair and fertile world given man for dwelling-place, truly an Eden (*land of delight*, as that word means) where the soft air was wafted laden with the fragrance of sweet flowers, where the birds warbled love-music, and the stream murmured its thanks for the jewels which the sunlight scattered on its bosom.

CHAPTER IV.

LEGENDS OF THE PAST ABOUT MANKIND.

To the legends already given may be added a few concerning the early state of mankind.

For thousands of years before the rudest kind of picture-writing was invented, the mind of man was busily speculating how that which he saw had come to pass, and not less, but rather more, would he wonder whence and how he himself had come; and out of that wonderment have grown the legends which have been handed down by old-world fathers to their children. These legends of a beginning, of the first man, and of a bright unflecked day whose glory had gone, legends in which a little fact was mixed up with much guessing, came to be looked upon as true every word, and were at last set down not as largely born of the fancy of man, but as history to be believed. And we find them lingering still among tribes and nations, because none readily give up the old for the new and cut themselves adrift from that which their fathers held dear.

Nearly all speak of happy times spent without labour or care, and then of evil stealing in and beguiling men with a lie. Seeking to explain the mystery of sorrow and pain, of the guilt and hard toil to which none are strangers, they have dreamed of a past when these ills were not. 'The Pârsî looks back to the happy rule of King Yima, when men and cattle were immortal, when water and trees never dried up and food was plentiful, when there was no cold nor heat, no envy nor old age. The Buddhist looks back to the age of glorious soaring beings who had no sin, no sex, no want of food till the unhappy hour when, tasting a delicious scum that formed upon the surface of the earth, they fell into evil and in time became degraded. It was King Chetiya who told the first lie, and the people who heard of it, not knowing what a lie was, asked if it were white or black or blue. Men's lives grew shorter and shorter, and it was King Maha Sâgara who, after a brief reign of two hundred and fifty-two thousand years, made the dismal discovery of the first grey hair.'

The Tibetans and Mongolians believe that the first human beings were as gods, but desiring a certain sweet herb, they ate of it, and lower feelings were thus aroused within them; their wings dropped off; their beauty faded; and the years of their life were made few and filled with bitterness. Passing by any full account of the Hindu story of a tree of life on a mountain ever bathed in sunshine, where no sin could enter and where dreadful dragons kept the way to the heavenly plants and fruits, and also of the Greek belief that far away there were the Islands of the Blessed with a garden full of golden apples guarded by an unsleeping serpent, we have the Greek myth which tells us that the first men were happy and without work, but with a desire to assert their power, and withal defy or mock the gods. Then Promêtheus shaped a human form out of clay, and stole forbidden fire from heaven wherewith to give it life. This made Zeus angry, and he laid a plan by which the evils that mankind dreaded, and which were sealed within a box guarded by Epimêtheus, the brother of Promêtheus, should be let loose. He ordered the lord of fire to fashion the first woman, who by her charms should bring misery to man. Then the gods enriched her with beauty, cunning and fair speech, naming her Pandôra or All-gifted, and Zeus took her to Epimêtheus who, contrary to the advice of his brother to accept nothing from the gods, made her his wife, so smitten was he with her beautiful face and so beguiled by her smooth words. She had not been long with him before she opened the box, from whence came forth strife and sickness and all other ills that afflict mankind, and then hastily closing it, she shut up hope within, so that no comfort was given to men.

In Persian tradition Ormuzd is said to have promised the first man and woman never-ending bliss if they would remain good. But a demon in the form of a serpent was sent by Ahriman, and they believed the lie he told them that the good gifts came from Ahriman, whom they thereupon worshipped. The demon then brought them fruits, which they ate, and thereby lost their happy state. Driven away, they killed beasts for food and wore their skins, and in the hearts of these unhappy creatures there raged hatred and envy, which cursed them and their children.

The likeness of this legend to that in Genesis which tells how woe befel Adam and Eve when, tempted by a talking serpent, they ate forbidden fruit, is very striking. Both may have preserved the memory of a time when men were driven by great changes of climate, summer's heat giving place to long winter's cold, into untrodden wilds; driven, as they thought, by the anger of an offended God.

The mention of a serpent in both these legends reminds us what a great part that creature has played in many religions as an object of worship; also as an emblem of both good and evil, as among the Persians and other Eastern nations; of wisdom, as among African and other tribes who believe that the souls of some ancestors pass into snakes; of eternity, when coiling itself in the form of a circle, as among the Egyptians and Phœnicians; and of dominion, under the shape of a dragon, as among the Chinese. Crawling on its belly (its name comes from the Latin, *serpo*, to creep) with stealthy, dart-like movement; with glittering eye that held the shuddering looker-on, as if spellbound; and with horrid hiss; no wonder that the strange reptile, so unlike beast or bird, came at last to be regarded in many lands as the symbol of evil, and that over its destruction feasts were held and sacrifices offered. That the legend of dire work wrought by it has found a place in Jewish writings is not matter for surprise, nor that people should make the common blunder of believing that it was the devil who under such a form beguiled Adam and Eve into disobedience.

Much could be said about the false beliefs to which this legend has given rise, but, happily, they are dying out, and we may pass them by and go on to see what truth underlies the ancient story of the fashioning of man.

In the first account of creation in the book of Genesis we read that 'God created man in his image, in the image of God created he him; male and female created he them.' The apostle Paul told the Greeks that 'as we are the offspring of God, we ought not to think that the Godhead is like unto gold or silver or stone graven by art and man's device,' and since we cannot think of Him Who is a Spirit, Who is everywhere, both in the heart of man and in the desert wilds, as having any form; or length, breadth and height; it is clear that these words in Genesis cannot be read by us as referring to the *body* of man, which has shape and form, but as referring to the *soul*, which is the man. The word *man* comes from a root which in Sanskrit means the *thinker*; and *soul* has the same meaning; each name an old-world witness to the greatness of the being who is nearer to the God above him than he is to the brutes below him. With these he has very much in common, and the knowledge of this should engender kindness towards them, but a great gulf, as it seems to me, divides the two. Brutes have not, in the strict meaning of the term as we use it, a moral sense, or voice within which speaks to them of the rightness or wrongness of what they do. They show love and hate, revenge, shame and pride, but they cannot commit *sin*, neither sink lower nor rise higher than they are. A hungry lion kills and eats a man, not for the mere love of killing, but to satisfy his hunger, for until the hunger returns, he will harm none of the creatures he preys upon. We do not say that the lion has done *wrong*, or that he *ought* not to have done such a thing, but we say that he has acted according to his *brute nature,* and we have outgrown the practice of past ages when animals and lifeless things were punished as criminals for evils which befel men through them.* But when men commit crimes, we say that they *ought* not so to do, and we treat them as beings who have the power to do right as well as the power to do wrong; the power to choose between a better and a worse, and thus rise nobly or fall shamefully.

In the second account of creation in Genesis, we read that 'the Lord God formed man of the dust of the ground and breathed into his nostrils the breath of life: and man became a living soul.'

Now the matter of which the universe has been formed has neither been added to nor lessened, and therefore it follows that at the birth of any living thing there is no bringing in of new matter, but the using over again of the old.

* See Note C.

Of the matter of which the earth is composed, the flower, the insect, the bird, the fish and the brute are alike made, and they live and grow and repair their waste by taking into themselves air and light and food. And the body of man is not something different from these, but one with them 'of the dust of the ground,' and in itself not more wonderfully formed for its purpose than they for their purpose. Whether in the long course of ages it has come through lower forms to be what it is, or was fashioned by itself, we cannot say, for men of science are not agreed about this hard question. Neither does it matter; 'that which we are we are,' and the query is not *whether* God has worked, giving to each moving thing 'a body as it hath pleased Him,' for of that we are sure; but *how* He has worked, concerning which we may be content to remain ignorant.

It is interesting to note that Science confirms in the main what is said in Genesis i. about the order in which life appeared upon the earth, since the deepest layers of rocks, which of course are the oldest, yield fossils of the lowest forms of life, forms so faint that whether they be the remains of plant or of animal, or of both, is uncertain; and the nearer we come to the surface the higher is the kind of life found to have been, until the highest of all, man himself, is reached, his presence being first shown in rudely chipped stone tools and weapons, and next by his remains. It may be added that the ancient Egyptians believed the first man to have been formed from the slime of the river Nile; the Chinese that he was shaped from yellow clay; the Peruvians that he was created by Divine power as 'animated earth;' one of the North American tribes that the Great Spirit formed two figures from clay, who were named 'first man' and 'companion;' another tribe says that men once lived underground, but that finding a hole through which to creep to the surface, they were tempted by the plentiful food to remain above ground.

CHAPTER V.

EARLY RACES OF MANKIND.

IT is believed that the birthplace of man was in some part of the earth where the climate was warm, so that but slight clothing and shelter were needed, and where food and the other gifts of Nature were so abundant, that life was no hard struggle.

The exact spot we may never know, but nearly all our present information points, as hinted at page 38, to some land now beneath the Indian Ocean.* The vast number of stone implements which have been found in Europe and many other parts of the globe were without doubt shaped by the hand of man many thousands of years ago; but although they give some clue to the rude, wild state of those who made them, they throw no light whatever on the question of man's first home. His greatness among all living creatures,

* See Note D.

from the earliest time of which we have glimpses, is seen in this: that although he was made naked and with a bodily frame much weaker than many of the brutes, he was able, armed only with clumsy stone weapons, to slay animals of a huge size. And this because as *brutes* they knew nothing of their own power, wherewith they could have crushed him with ease; while as *man* he had the knowledge whereby so to use his weapons as to subdue and kill them.

Let us see whether the records of changes in Europe throw any light upon man's arrival there.

If we find imbedded in layers of rock the remains of animals and plants which could live only in hot regions, we may fairly conclude what the climate must have been when they flourished.

Now from the nature of the fossils found in what are called the Tertiary rocks (from Lat. *tertius*, third), which compose the *third* great division of the water-laid rocks, it is certain that the climate of Europe was once very warm. Thick jungles and tangled forest-growths of plants akin to those in hot countries abounded, amongst which creatures of huge size and vast numbers roamed at will, crunching the young shoots and branches between their enormous teeth; while the river-creeks and swamps were the abode of wallowing crocodiles, sharks and turtles of monster size.

In those rocks no remains of man in bones or stone implements have been found.

After this a season of the bitterest cold, known as the Ice Age, slowly set in, and covered with thick plates of ice the northern parts of the earth. While this was going on, the continent of Europe, which had stretched beyond Ireland, gradually sank beneath the sea, so that a large part of it was changed into frozen straits and many ice-clad islands. In the long course of time the climate again became milder and the land 'arose from out the azure main,' so that Ireland was re-united to Britain, and Britain to the mainland, which was joined to Africa at different parts, the Mediterranean Sea being thereby divided into two large land-locked basins. Periods of cold and heat followed one another; at one time the woolly-haired rhinoceros, mammoth or maned elephant, cave-bear and other wild beasts lived here, and when warmer times drove them to more northern parts, hippopotamuses, lions, hyenas and such like tenants of hot countries came.

It should be stated that there are seen to be three well-marked divisions of the great reign of cold, and it is not certain whether man had reached Europe before the first and most severe Ice Age set in, although certain relics which tend to prove that he had, have been lately found in caverns. The earliest traces of him are the stone tools and weapons found in ancient river-valleys and mingled with the remains of animals, of a kind long since extinct, that roamed over the north-west when there was dry land between England and France, and when a wide plain over which the North Sea now sweeps stretched from Norfolk to Belgium.

That the makers of these old stone implements must have lived in Britain many hundred thousand years ago is proved by the finding of tools of the rudest shape in the floors of limestone caverns which have been scooped out of the rock by the slow action of water. The limy matter in or beneath which the implements are found imbedded and which is called stalagmite (from Greek *stalagma*, a drop) is formed as follows. Rain water passes through the limestone roof, and by means of the carbonic acid which it has derived from the air and from decayed leaves and the like, eats away particles of the roof through which it trickles and drops them beneath as carbonate of lime or *stalagmite*. Sometimes the dissolved particles cling to the roof and hanging from it form in course of time very beautiful columns called *stalactites*, but with these we have nothing to do.

Now as the rate at which the stalagmite is laid down gives some clue to the age of the relics found beneath it when there is proof that it has not been disturbed, it will be well to enter one of the most famous caverns situate near Torquay, known as 'Kent's Hole,' and see for ourselves of what age the several deposits doubtless are.

First, there are blocks of limestone, which have fallen from the roof from time to time.

Then black muddy mould, beneath which lies a bed of stalagmite varying from three inches to five feet in thickness. Underneath this are two layers, one only a few inches thick and composed mainly of charred wood; the other some feet in thickness and composed of earth which has been slowly washed in through the cavern's mouth. Then we come to a second bed of stalagmite of a different character to the upper bed, and much thicker than it, reaching in some parts to a depth of twelve feet. Below all these lies a dark red sandy deposit called *breccia* (Italian, meaning a *fragment*) the depth of which is unknown.

In the uppermost layer there were found relics of a time before the Romans invaded Britain, which we may safely put down as 2000 years old. In the upper stalagmite there were found bones of the rhinoceros, elephant, hyena, &c., and of man, with flakes struck off flints by human hands and also the cores from which they had been struck. Now without going farther down at present, how can we get at the age of this stalagmite? There have been cut into it certain letters and dates, one of which—'Robert Hedges, of Ireland, Feb. 20, 1688'—we may believe is genuine, because it was discovered just 50 years ago, on a huge boss of stalagmite rising up from the floor; and although there are others of earlier date, we will take it as our point of reckoning. It is described by the man who saw it in 1825 as covered over with a thin film of stalagmite, a description which applies to it now, although the water has been dripping on it ever since.

Now the carbonate of lime which has gathered upon that cutting since 1688 does not exceed the *twentieth of an inch* in thickness, and we have to account for a deposit which is in some places *five feet* thick. By an easy sum in multiplication we find that it takes 3720 years for the water trickling through the roof of Kent's Hole to deposit *one inch* of stalagmite, and therefore 44,640 years to deposit *one foot*. Five feet consequently require two hundred and twenty-three thousand years!

But we have not done yet. There is the layer of charred wood, called the 'black band' which yielded hundreds of flint tools, a bone needle, burnt bones, remains of hyenas, bears, oxen, &c. There is the cave earth with relics of a like kind, and then we come to the lower bed of stalagmite, which contained bones of the cave-bear only, and which is in some places more than double the thickness of the upper bed, and requiring at the least five hundred thousand years for its formation!

It is underneath this that in the solid mass called breccia there were found mingled with immense numbers of teeth and bones of the cave-bear, flint implements, which without doubt were shaped by the hand and skill of man. Enormous as these figures are, I have been careful to understate rather than overstate them, for there are proofs that within this same cavern an inch of stalagmite is not laid down by water in less than 5000 years, at which rate the time needed for the deposit of the upper bed alone is three hundred thousand years!

The thickness of layers of stalagmite is not always a test of the great age of remains found in them or below them, as in some caverns they are formed at a very much quicker rate than in others, and if the proof of man's early presence on the earth rested on this alone, it would be needful to speak with caution. But further proof is at hand in the worked flints found in the river-gravels of England and France, and in the kind of animals with whose remains his own are found, that man lived in northern Europe towards the close of the later Ice Age, if not earlier, and therefore hundreds of thousands of years ago; although the actual time of his arrival can never be known.

We do not know to what race the men who first trod the soil of Europe belonged. They came with the mammoth, cave-bear, &c., and we cannot tell whither they went. There is, however, some clue to those who followed them. These were dwellers in caves, living chiefly on the flesh of the reindeer, which creature they hunted as far as the northern land of bitter cold, where the snow never melts and the blessed light shines but six months in the year. The manners and customs and general kind of life of the tribes found there at this day, known as the Eskimos, are so very like all that can be learnt about the old cave-men of what is called the Reindeer Period, that there is good reason for believing that the one is descended from the other.

After a time which years fail to reckon, when the waters, ever working 'without haste and without rest,' had cut a channel between England and France, there came to Europe from the East race after race of people who were far higher than the cave-men. The lowest among them, of whom traces are found along the shores of the Baltic Sea, had tamed the dog, while those who lived in houses built upon piles driven into the bottom of lakes in Switzerland and elsewhere, had learnt to till the soil.

Mankind at first were few in number, but as the mouths to be fed multiplied faster than the food wherewith to fill them, it was needful either that the ground should be tilled or that some should leave in search of food elsewhere, and since man must advance somewhat before he becomes a husbandman, the latter course would be chosen.

So, hunger-driven or forced away by change of climate, and also, it may be, led on by desire to see what the world was like and to find excitement in chasing animals to kill and eat, some would leave, and thus give up a settled kind of life, which tends to peaceful progress, for a roving life. The pressing wants of the body urged them to wander far and wide, and soon long distances would divide the hunters. This would lead to the peopling of the world in many parts, and in the course of long ages to the fixing of wandering tribes wherever food was to be had, and the land seemed fair and fertile.

From this we may understand how the earliest dwellers in Europe were driven thither. They were but rude savages, living by hunting and fishing. Man is first of all a hunter, then he finds out that some of the animals which he kills for food can be made useful to him in other ways, so he tames them. This leads him to follow the more settled life of a shepherd, and when he becomes a tiller of the soil, or farmer, he stays in one place. There the family grows into a tribe and the tribe into a nation.

Thus far I hope to have made clear to you the mode in which mankind slowly overspread various parts of the world, and I have now to give you, in as simple a form as the subject will permit, an account of some ancient peoples who have played a markedly eventful part in the history of mankind.

I shall take you back to the time when man had outgrown his first rude savage state; but, so many are the years, we shall still be a long way beyond the line where the history of nations stands out clearly before us. The story is worth your careful attention, for to know who these peoples were and what they did, is to learn the thoughts of ancestors whose words we speak and to find out how we have become what we are.

The old writers, in speaking of 'the world,' took for granted that it did not extend beyond the countries of which they knew. Now although its real size and shape are well known to us, we are too apt to think only of that part of it where the highest races have lived, and to leave out the other parts with their millions of people still in a savage or half-civilized state. This must be borne in mind in reading what follows, since the limits of this book forbid my stating what is known of the manner of life and religions of the numerous races scattered over the northern regions of Asia, over large tracts of Africa and America, and throughout the many islands of the southern seas.

It is certain that the people to be presently described were not the first civilizers, but were young as compared to Egypt and China, and built up much of their future greatness out of the ruins of more ancient cultures. For apart from the rude savages whose early struggles made progress easier to those who came after them, there are found over wide regions of Europe and Asia the traces of a people who have immensely helped the advancement of mankind. I am now speaking of the ancestors of the great Mongol race, of the Tatars (wrongly called Tartars) and of the many tribes of Northern Asia, of Southern India, Malay, and other parts of South-western Asia; also of the Finns, Lapps, Hungarians and smaller remnants, such as the Basque dwellers in the Pyrenees, lingering in out-of-the-way places.

Many of these have preserved the manners, customs and beliefs of a bygone day, and having reached a certain point, seem to have stood still while the rest of the world has moved onward. The history of mankind is made up of struggles between races in which the weaker have been stamped out or enslaved, but these people, whose forefathers were by turns conquerors and conquered, are amongst us, many of them free and independent, still worshipping the heavenly bodies and the spirits of their ancestors as did their forefathers thousands of years âgo.

CHAPTER VI.

THE ARYAN OR INDO-EUROPEAN NATIONS.

THOUSANDS of years ago there dwelt probably in Central Asia, scattered over the wide plains which spread east of the Caspian sea and north-west of Hindustan, a number of tribes united together by the same manners and customs, and speaking somewhat different dialects of a common tongue, in short, the offspring of one mother-nation.

These tribes consisted of two great branches, from one of which have come the races that have peopled nearly the whole of Europe; that is to say, the Celts (whom Julius Cæsar found in Britain when he invaded it); the Germans and Slavonians; the Greeks and Romans; while from the other branch the Medes, Persians and Hindus, with some lesser peoples in Asia, have sprung.

A learned German has called this 'the discovery of a new world.' And it is certainly a great revelation to us that the Hindu and the Icelander;

the Russian and the Italian; the Englishman and the Frenchman; are children whose forefathers lived in one home. A knowledge of this fact must aid the growth of kindlier feeling between man and man, and lessen the unreasoning dislike which we are apt to nurture against foreigners.

So true is it that 'God hath made of one blood all nations of men for to dwell on all the face of the earth, and hath determined the times before appointed and the bounds of their habitation; that they should seek the Lord, if haply they might feel after him and find him, though he be not far from every one of us.'

Ârya is a Sanskrit word, meaning *noble*, of a *good family*. It is believed to have come from the root *ar*, to plough, which is found in *era*, the Greek word for *earth*; *earth* meaning that which is *eared* or ploughed. We find the word so used in Tusser, an early English poet, who says,

'Such land as ye break up for barley to sow,
Two *earths* at the least, ere ye sow it, bestow.'

That is, plough it twice. And in Isaiah xxx. 24, we read of 'the oxen and the young asses that *ear* the ground.' *Aryan* was the name given to the tillers of the soil and to householders, and the title by which the once famous Medes and Persians were proud to call themselves. We find King Darius styling himself an Arya of the Aryans. It became a general name for the race who obtained possession of the land, and survives in *Iran*, the modern native name of Persia and in other names of places; even, as some think, in Ireland, which is called *Erin* by the natives. The name *Indo-European* is sometimes used instead of *Aryan,* and it is a better name because it conveys a clearer idea of the races included therein.

We will now enquire more fully into the old life of this interesting people, first treating of them in their common home, which will cause something more to be said about legends of the past; then of their arts and customs; the source from whence comes our knowledge of them; their religion; their myths, from which, as already hinted in the opening pages of this book, most of the myths and legends and even some beliefs of the chief nations of Europe, have come ; and lastly, of the breaking-up of the tribes, when the children went forth, heaven-guided, to plant the seed from which grew empires that have been the wonders of the world. Such survey will bring us near the time when some great religions had their rise, and of these an account will fitly follow.

(a) THE ARYANS IN THEIR UNDIVIDED STATE.

In the Zend-Avesta, or sacred book of the old Persian religion, only fragments of which have been preserved, there are some statements about the country peopled by the Aryans which seem to hold a little truth.

Sixteen countries are spoken of as having been given by Ormuzd for the Aryans to dwell in, each of which became tainted with evil. The first was named Airyanem-Vaêgô and it was created a land of delight, but, to quote the ancient legend 'the evil being Ahriman, full of death, made a mighty serpent and winter, the work of the Devas' (or bad spirits).

The land thus vaguely spoken of is believed to

be the highest ground in Central Asia, and to have been the scene of changes which gave rise to a cold climate with but two months of summer in the year. In this Persian legend we have one of the many traditions which have come down from the past concerning disaster and ruin befalling fair lands where men once dwelt in peace. The most widespread of these, being in fact found among all the leading races of the world, is that which tells of a fearful flood which drowned mankind. The sea-shells and fossil fishes imbedded in rocks now many hundreds of feet above the level of the sea could only be accounted for by supposing either that the sea once came up and covered the highest hills, leaving its wrecks behind; or that the mountains had been down in the sea; and as the former seemed the more likely of the two, the tradition took that shape.

I shall have to resist the temptation to relate many of these traditions, but the Chaldæan must be told because of its striking likeness to the record of the Flood in the Book of Genesis. There are in fact two Chaldæan accounts of the Deluge, one of which, belonging to a series of legends on tablets found among the ruins of Nineveh, has of late come to light, and resembles that now given.

It is said that the god Ilu (see page 201) warned Xisuthrus of a flood by which mankind would be destroyed, and commanded him to write a history of all things and to bury it in the City of the Sun. He was then to build a ship, and take refuge in it with his relations and friends, and also every kind of beast and bird, with needful food for all. This he did, and when the flood came sailed as he was bidden ' to the gods.' That he might know whether the waters had abated, he sent out birds three times, and the third time they came back no more, by which he judged that the earth was again dry land. Looking out from a window he found that the ship had stranded upon the side of some mountain, and he thereupon quitted it with his wife and daughter. After worshipping the earth and offering sacrifice to the gods, he was translated to live in their high dwelling-place, and as he arose he bade farewell to those whom he had left in the ship, and told them to return to Babylon and dig up the books which he had buried. This they did, and taught from those books the true religion to the Chaldæans.

The Babylonians and the Jews were members of the same race, and this may explain the likeness between their traditions. Thus the Chaldæan records speak of the building of the Tower of Babel, the legend of which has just been found on another tablet from Nineveh, how the first inhabitants of the earth, glorying in their own strength and size and despising the gods, undertook to raise a tower whose top should reach the sky in the place where Babylon now stands, but when it approached the heaven, the winds helped the gods, and overthrew the work upon its builders; then the gods confused the speech of men, who till that time had all spoken the same language. The Bible gives *ten* patriarchs who lived before the flood, each of whom died at a great age, and the Chaldæan history speaks of *ten* kings whose reigns, added together, amount to 432,000 years, while in Arab, Chinese, Hindu and German legend, *ten* mythical persons are said to have lived before the dawn of history. So strongly runs the likeness between the old traditions, a likeness to be expected, since they are the children of one parent. That parent was the busy, wonder-filled mind of man, when it shaped the creatures of its fancy out of the facts around; creatures that have found a home among every people.

You must read elsewhere the story of the Northern giants who were sent to overturn the earth, and who drowned all mankind save an old couple whom the gods told to dance on the bones of the earth (by which of course the *stones* are meant) nine times, whence arose nine pairs of men and women; of the Greek and his wife who, when the flood came, took refuge in an ark and leaving it when the land was dry, threw stones behind them, which were thereupon changed into men; of the Hindu who saved the life of a fish, for which kind deed the grateful creature rescued him, when the great waters came, by fastening his ship to its horn; and of the South Sea fisherman who by ill luck caught his hooks in the water-god's hair, which so angered the god that he drowned the world, but, strange to say, spared the fisherman.

Leaving the legends, it would seem that the Aryans had gradually spread themselves over that part of Asia called Bactria; the tribes that afterwards settled in Persia and India dwelling, some in the north-east, others in the south-east; while the western part of the country was occupied by the tribes that were to people Europe. We shall see at the end of this chapter in what order they are thought to have left.

(b) THEIR STATE OF CIVILIZATION.

Of the forefathers of the Aryans nothing is known. Remains yielded by every quarter of the globe show that mankind passed through a state when the rudest and roughest tools were gladly used, and there can be little doubt that although the Aryans had learnt the value of metals, they were the offspring of people who had in a far-off past made shift with stone, bone, wood, and such like materials. At the unknown period when the Aryans dwelt on the rich pastures and fertile soil of their high table-land they were far in advance of a savage state. They were not dwellers in tents like the Arabs, nor in waggons like the Scythians, but they had reached the settled life of a people whose dwellings were grouped into villages or small towns, between which roads had been made. Their houses were strongly built, with walls round them. Their chief wealth was in bulls and cows, and they had horses, dogs, pigs, goats, fowls, &c. In fact, the wild stocks of several of our domestic animals still exist in Central Asia, from whence they were brought by the Aryans into Europe. They did not depend entirely for food upon milk and flesh, but tilled the soil a little, sowing barley, and perhaps wheat, which they ground in mills. They had ploughs and other implements, and also weapons of bronze. Gold, silver and copper were known among them, but probably iron was as yet unknown. The arts of weaving and pottery-making were practised, and they had small boats moved by oars, but without masts and sails. They had learnt to count as far as one hundred, and to divide the year into twelve months, as suggested chiefly by the movements of the moon. Names were given to the members of families related by marriage as well as by blood. A welcome greeted the birth of children as of those who brought joy to the home, and the love that should be felt between brother and sister was shewn in the names given; *bhrâtar* being he who *sustains* or *helps*; *svâsar*, she who *pleases* or *consoles*. The daughter of each household was called *duhitár*, from *duh*, a root which in Sanskrit means *to milk*, by which we know that the girls in those days were the *milking maids*. Father comes from a root *pâ*, which means to *protect* or *support*; mother, *mâtar*, has the meaning of *maker*. Thus did the old words carry within them the sense of those duties which each member of the family owed to the rest.

The groups of families which made up a tribe or clan were ruled by a chief, aided by heads of households, and under these the laws were carried out. A king was set over all; one doubtless chosen for his bravery and wisdom, who commanded the army and made peace or war. He was also supreme judge, but any cases upon which he felt it hard to decide were settled by what is called *ordeal* or the judgment of God, as it was believed to be. That the innocence or guilt of an accused person might be arrived at, he had to submit to some test, such as being passed through fire (from which comes our phrase about any one who has been scolded; we say he has been 'hauled over the coals'), or thrown into water, and, in the words of the law-book of the ancient Hindus, 'he whom the flame does not burn and he who does not float without effort on the water, must be accepted as truthful.' Trial by ordeal was common among ancient nations, and was supported by both law and clergy in the dark ages of Europe.

(c) SOURCE OF OUR KNOWLEDGE ABOUT THE ARYANS.

Ethnology (from Greek *ethnos*, a tribe or nation, and *logos*, a discourse) is the name given to the science which treats of the races of mankind. Our present knowledge strengthens the early belief that man first arose in one part of the earth, but the result of many causes, such as changes in climate, removal to new lands, different food, working through long ages, has been to create wide varieties in his descendants, such as we see between an Englishman and a Negro, and between a Hindu and a Chinaman. In dividing mankind into races, men of science have tried many methods, tracing out likeness in shape and size of skull, in colour of skin and hair, in manners, customs and beliefs, in language, &c., but no one of these has succeeded in accounting for all the varieties in the human race.

What immense service one of these methods has been will now appear.

The Aryans, whose manner of life has been sketched in its main features, have left behind them no ruins of temples or tombs, no history stamped on pieces of baked clay or cut on rocks, no weapons or tools of stone, bone or metal, so far as is known, and it is by means of LANGUAGE alone that we can rebuild the villages of the old Aryan land and bring before the mind some picture of life in them thousands of years ago.

When a bone with scratchings upon it is dug from out a cavern floor, there may be room for doubt whether the hand of a man working with stone tool, or the teeth of a brute, have made the marks; but wherever we find *words* there is no doubt that man has used them: and it was through them that the secret about these Aryan forefathers came to light.

There were seen to be so many points of likeness between certain languages which could be accounted for only by supposing those languages to be the offspring of one mother-tongue. This likeness was noticed in the homely words and common names which make up so much of the speech of everyday life; it was most marked in the numerals and pronouns; and, what is of greater importance, in the forms of grammar;— the endings of nouns and verbs; the adding of the letter *s* to form plurals, &c.

As language is 'a map of the science and manners of the people who speak it,' the thing for which a name exists must have been known, and if it be found with the same name among nations widely apart and between whom there has been no meeting for ages, we have fair proof that their ancestors once lived together and used the thing. If we find a common name for *house, boat, plough, grain,* in Sanskrit, Greek, and other leading languages, we may be nearly certain that these things were known to the tribes before they parted, whereas if the name for *sea* differs, it follows that the Aryans were an inland race and knew nothing of the wide waters that laved the distant coasts. There is further proof of this in the smallness of their skiffs or canoes, which it is clear were for river use, since, as already stated, they had no masts or sails.

There are certain differences in the words, arising from the changes to which the sounds of a language are liable, one sound being often used in the place of another, as is the case, for example, with children in trying to utter certain words. These changes were found to have taken place upon a large scale in all the Indo-European languages, and their nature is now fully known and set forth in modern grammars. They are grouped together under the title of 'Grimm's Law,' from the name of their discoverer.

It is true it does not follow that the English and Germans are of the same race because their languages are so much alike, for there are cases in history where a people, without any change in itself, has lost its mother-tongue and spoken the language of its conquerors, but this has taken place only when it has been so entirely subdued as to be civilized by the victors, as for example when the Romans conquered Gaul and wellnigh stamped out the Gaulish speech, putting Latin in its place. This, however, does not apply to the Aryan nations in their wars with non-Aryan races.

Before giving a list of the languages known to be offshoots from one parent stem, it may be well to explain that language is everywhere found to be in one of the three following states:

First, When roots, by which is meant sounds from which all languages spring, are used as words without any change of form.

Secondly, When two roots are joined together to form words.

Thirdly, When two roots are joined together, but when they, thus joined, lose their independent form.

The Chinese language, which consists of words of one syllable, is the best living example of language in its *first* stage, and beyond which, it is held by a few learned men, some languages never rise, however long they may live.

The Finnic, Hungarian, &c., languages represent language in its *second* stage.

The Aryan and Semitic languages represent language in its *third* and highest stage.

This example will show the change which the roots of certain languages undergo:

  First state . . He is *like God.*
  Second state . He is *God-like.*
  Third state . . He is *God-ly.*

Table of Aryan or Indo-European Languages.

In India:—

 Sanskrit, The language in which the Vedas or sacred books of the Brahmans are written, and the parent of the modern dialects of Hindustan.

 Zend,. . The language of the ancient Persians (so-called.) and of their sacred book, the Zend-Avesta.

The languages now spoken in Persia, Afghanistan, Kurdistan, Armenia and Ceylon, and the dialects of the *Gypsies* are Aryan, those strange wanderers having without doubt come from India

In Europe :—

Celtic, . Once the language of a large part of Europe, but now spoken only in Wales, the Isle of Man, and some parts of Ireland and Scotland.

Teutonic, Under which name the languages that have given birth to the English, German, Icelandic, Danish, Norwegian, Swedish, Dutch, &c., are grouped.

Slavonic, The language spoken in many dialects all over Russia in Europe and part of Austria.

Greek, . The parent of modern Greek.

Latin, . The language of ancient Rome (which was in the little province of *Latium*) and the parent of the Italian, French, Spanish, Portuguese and Wallachian languages.

No one of these can be pointed out as the source from which the others have come, because although Sanskrit has preserved its words in their most primitive state, each of the others has also kept some form which Sanskrit has lost. It is one of the few *facts* of history that before the Hindus crossed the mountains that lay between Bactria and India, and before the Celts and other tribes left for the west, their common ancestors spoke the same language; a language so firmly settled that Sanskrit, Persian, Greek, Latin, Germanic, Slavonic and Celtic words are simply *alterations* of its words and not *additions* to it. A few plain examples will best make this clear, and close what some of you will call the driest chapter in the book.

	Sanskrit.	*Zend.*	*Greek.*	*Latin.*	*Gothic.*	*Slavonic.*	*Irish.*
Father .	pitár	patar	patêr	pater	fadar	...	athair
Mother .	mátár	mâtar	mêtêr	mater	...	mati	mathair
Brother .	bhrâtar	brâtar	phratêr	frater	brôthar	brat'	brathair
Sister . .	svásar	qanhar	...	soror	svistar	sestra	siur
Daughter	duhitar	dughdhar	thugater	...	dauhtar	...	dear (?)
Me . . .	me	me	me	me	mik	man	me
House .	dama	demana	domos	domus	...	domü	daimh
Boat . .	naus	naw	naus	navis	...	...	noi or nai
Ox & Cow	go (nom. gaus)	gâo	bous	bos	...	govjado	bó
Horse .	âsu, asva	aspa	hippos	equus	*Anglo-Saxon.* eoh	...	ech
Sow . .	sû	...	hus	sus	*Old High German.* sû	*Polish.* svinia	suig
Mouse .	mûsh	...	mus	mus	mûs	mysz	...
Two . .	dwa	dwa	dúo	duo	*Moeso-Gothic.* twa	*Slavonic.* dwa	dau
Three . .	tri	thri	treis	treis	thri	tri	tri

I have sought to make this matter simple enough that you may see how language is filled with wealth of knowledge about the past, and how sure a guide it is to the manners, customs and beliefs of those who 'being dead, yet speak' by it.

(d.) THE RELIGION OF THE ARYANS.

In the second part of my former book, 'The Childhood of the World,' I tried to show by what steps man rose from the worship of sticks and stones and rivers, to a belief in one all-wise and all-good God. It is not needful to go over that ground again, as in learning from whence the Aryan drew his idea of the gods, we shall see to what extent he had got beyond the lower beliefs of his ancestors. He had not reached the highest idea to which man can climb, that God is the unseen life of all and that 'there is none other but he,' for his belief was shaped from what he saw.

Before the notions about things which the senses give had been corrected by reason and the long experience of mankind, man explained the movements of nature by his own movements. He knew that he moved because he lived and willed to do whatever he did, and that the dead moved not. So he believed that sun, moon, stars, clouds, rivers and the like, had life within them because they moved, and that theirs was a freer, stronger life than his own; obeying a will more powerful than his will. By a short step the thing spoken of as alive came to be looked upon as a person, and where two or more names were given to the same object the idea of two or more persons sprang therefrom. The spread of this idea would be aided by the division of lifeless things thus believed to have a personal life into masculine or feminine gender, of which some languages afford such curious and, to those who are learning them, tedious illustrations.

Although the Aryan addressed the earth as 'mother,' and invoked her to grant him blessings, he did not regard it as a god. How much there was in it to arouse his sense of wonder it is not hard for us to see, but it appeared to him to depend, like himself, upon some greater powers who could plunge it in darkness or withhold from its thirsty soil the welcome rain. So he looked up to the broad heaven that arched in the earth at every point, and from whence came each morning the light that cheered his life and took away the fear with which the night filled his heart. And there, so it seemed to him, lived and moved in strength and majesty the great lord of all, whom he named *Dyaus*, from a root *div* or *dyu*, which means *to shine*. This was the most ancient of the names by which the Aryans spoke of him who seemed the god of gods, and it is the name by which you and I often speak of the one God in Whom we believe, for it was borne away with other cherished home-words by the tribes when they left their mother-country, and as wherever they went the same heaven was above them, it was not readily forgotten. *Dyaus* is the same as *Zeus* in Greek; *Jovis* and *Deus* in Latin; and *Tiu* in German. From *Deus* comes our word *Deity*, which therefore means the God Who is light, and from *Tiu*, Saxon god of war, comes our *Tuesday*. In the Rig-Veda or chief sacred book of the Brahmans, the hymns of which have preserved the earliest known form of the Aryan religion, the gods are called *deva*, meaning *bright*.

Dyaus, the god of the bright sky and chief

deity among the Aryans, was, as will be seen in the chapter on the older Hindu religion, only one of several names by which they invoked the moving powers of nature. The same name was given to different objects in the heavens, and the same object was called by as many names as the fancy of the onlooker invented. As the powers of nature came to be thought of as persons, it was by an easy step that they were called husband and wife, mother and son, brother and sister. It was long ago a beautiful and forceful myth among mankind, and one still found among races in the myth-making stage, that heaven and earth are the father and mother of all things. Upon this matter a great light is thrown by the name *Jupiter*. This word means what in the Veda *Dyaus-pítar*, and in the Greek *Zeu-pater*, mean—Heaven-Father! Professor Max Müller, who has the rare gift of putting into sweetest words things that to the common eye look the driest, writes thus about this most interesting fact:—

'We have in the Veda the invocations *Dyaus-pítar*, the Greek Ζεῦπάτερ, the Latin *Jupiter*: and that means in all the three languages what it meant before these three languages were torn asunder—it means Heaven-Father! These two words are not mere words; they are to my mind the oldest poem, the oldest prayer of mankind, or at least of that pure branch of it to which we belong —and I am as firmly convinced that this prayer was uttered, that this name was given to the unknown God before Sanskrit was Sanskrit, and Greek was Greek, as when I see the Lord's Prayer in the languages of Polynesia and Melanesia, I feel certain that it was first uttered in the language of Jerusalem. We little thought when we heard for the first time the name of Jupiter, degraded it may be by Homer or Ovid into a scolding husband or a faithless lover, what sacred records lay enshrined in this unholy name. We shall have to learn the same lesson again and again in the Science of Religion, viz., that the place whereon we stand is holy ground. Thousands of years have passed since the Aryan nations separated to travel to the North and the South, the West and the East: they have each formed their languages, they have each founded empires and philosophies, they have each built temples and razed them to the ground; they have all grown older, and it may be wiser and better; but when they search for a name for what is most exalted and yet most dear to every one of us, when they wish to express both awe and love, the infinite and the finite, they can but do what their old fathers did when gazing up to the eternal sky, and feeling the presence of a Being as far as far and as near as near can be; they can but combine the self-same words, and utter once more the primeval Aryan prayer, Heaven-Father, in that form which will endure for ever, 'Our Father which art in heaven.'

Besides having common names for their chief gods, the Aryans had words to express the duties which they felt must be fulfilled towards the powers whose smiles they coveted and whose frowns they feared; as *sacrifice, prayer, altar, spirit.*

Sacrifice is the oldest of all rites. Man's first feeling towards the gods was that of fear. They ruled over all things, life and death were in their hands, and therefore it seemed needful to offer them something to win their favour. When he saw that the blessings of heaven outnumbered the ills, fear gave place to love, and *thank-offerings* were made. As the feeling grew that the gods must be better as well as stronger, the desire to have their forgiveness for bad deeds done and for good deeds left undone led to *sin-offerings*.

And as the sense of a common need was stronger than any other tie that bound the family together, the father, as its head, built the altar and laid the gift upon it. These gifts of things which could be seen and touched were a simple, and in fact the only, mode by which man could show the feeling of his heart, but in course of time the first meaning of the gifts was lost and they were looked upon not merely as *showing* something, but as *being* something. The place where the altar stood was revered, there men raised a temple (so called from the Latin *templum*, which means *a space cut off*), and a class of men grew up who made easy claim to power with the gods which they said was not given to all men. Thus religious rites, which were believed to have certain charms about them, were done by the priests only, and two great evils thereby came about. First;

people believed that the priests knew more about the unseen than other men, and so, leaving religion to them, gave up *thinking;* ceased to use the greatest gift which made them men. How frightfully this has kept the world back, we have the saddest proofs even to-day, in our forgetfulness that the voices of God are around us; that His secrets are not with any one class of men, but with them that fear Him, with them that are true to what they feel to be highest and best, whoever they may be. Next; the belief that certain buildings are more sacred than others, and that one kind of work is holier than another, has caused people to think that God is more with the priest than He is with the peasant, and more likely to be present in a church than in a house or a shop. The Psalmist knew better than that, for he asked, 'Whither shall I go from Thy spirit? or whither shall I flee from Thy presence?' And so did Jesus when he told the people that to the pure in heart there was some showing of God's blessed face, and that not on mountain or in city only, but everywhere He could be worshipped. The earth is a temple, and all honest work is service therein.

Sacrifice was an important part of the Aryan religion. A rude altar of turf or stones was piled upon some high place under the open sky, and the wood laid upon it was kindled by rubbing two dried branches together. One chief offering to the gods was the fermented juice of the Soma or moon-plant, which, being a strong drink, gave a new excitement to those who took it, and was believed to impart power to the gods. It was offered to them in ladles, or thrown into the fire. It was thought to work miracles, and afterwards became one of the chief gods among the Hindus. In a Vedic hymn the worshippers say—

> 'We've quaffed the Soma bright,
> And are immortal grown;
> We've entered into light,
> And all the gods have known.
> What mortal now can harm,
> Or foeman vex us more?
> Through thee, beyond alarm,
> Immortal God! we soar.'

(See also page 142).

Other gifts, such as butter (produce of the

valued cow), grains of barley, cakes, &c., were presented, and at solemn seasons animals were offered, the highest sacrifice being that of the horse, which creature was a frequent victim among the Scandinavians. Tacitus tells us that among the Teutons sacred white horses never ridden by men, were kept in groves, and fed at the public cost.

The Veda gives an insight into the hymns and prayers used at these sacrifices, and the *Vach*, or 'Goddess of Speech,' who taught the people to worship in spirit as well as in form, is praised in words which are very like those about Wisdom in the 8th chapter of Proverbs:—

'I uphold both the sun and the moon, the firmament and fire. I am queen and mistress of riches, I am wise. Listen then to me, for I speak words worthy of belief. Whom I love I make holy and wise. . . . I pervade heaven and earth. I bore the father on the head of this (universal mind), and my beginning is in the midst of the ocean; therefore do I pervade all beings, and touch this heaven with my form. I breathe in all worlds; I am above this heaven, beyond this earth; and what is the great one, that am I.'

This brief sketch of Aryan religion, especially the early notions of virtue and divine power abiding in the Soma, shows us a truth which is every day becoming clearer; that the things which are thought to belong only to one religion are common to all religions. The Roman Catholic priest who elevates the consecrated bread called the 'host' (from Latin *hostia*, a victim), is after all but an imitator of the old Aryan worshipper who, when he offered the Soma, raised the wooden cup that held it.

(e) ARYAN MYTHS.

You know that there is found among every people what is called a *mythology* (from Greek *muthos*, a fable, and *logos*, a word), under which name may be classed all legends and traditions, and also the fairy tales to which boys and girls listen so eagerly. There is common to myth and folk-lore the stories of the loves and quarrels of gods and goddesses, the feasts they ate, and the foes they slew; of heroes fighting with monsters for the rescue of fair maidens from dark dungeons and enchanted castles, of love-sick princes crossing wide seas in quest of the princess whom they wish to marry, and doing many deeds of daring to win her; of brave and cunning dwarfs that kill greedy, cruel and stupid giants; of strange creatures that lived in forest, in stream and underneath the ground—in Northern lands, known as nixies or water-sprites; as trolls or hill-dwarfs; as golden-haired elves that come from Elf-home at moonlight to dance in fairy rings upon the grass and make the air gently tremble with the soft music of their magic harps; in Southern lands, the naiades or water-nymphs, the satyrs and fauns and pigmies—and, all the world over, the beings too many to name, that dwell in wonder-land. Then there are the legends that people the air with the spirits of the dead, with sheeted ghosts, thirsty vampires, witches and the like; that tell of strange powers for good or evil possessed by living and lifeless things, of men changed into bears and wolves and stones; of maidens changed into swans; of waters of life and death and forgetfulness; of magic horns, lamps, cudgels, table-cloths and necklaces; of flasks that fill the ocean and talismans that open hidden stores of gold and gems; legends accounting for the cross on the ass's back, the marks on the haddock, the bear's stumpy tail, the robin's red breast, the wasp's narrow waist, the echoes among the hills, the saltness of the sea, the spots on the moon, and so on. We must also include as more or less out-growths of myth the great Epics (or poems describing the deeds of heroes) of the Aryan nations; in Norseland the tales of the Volsungs; in England, the tales of King Arthur and his Round Table Knights; in Greece, the Iliad and Odyssey; and the minor stories which are found among many peoples, such as the skill of Tell the archer, and the mistake of the prince who slew the faithful dog Gellert, that had saved his child from the wolf. Now, strange to tell, just as the languages of the English, Russians, Hindus and other Aryan nations have come from one source, so also have many of their myths, legends and fairy tales. It is worth your while to hear how this has been found out.

Much that was passed by in former years as meaningless and unworthy of notice has in our day been looked at with care and found to be full of history and meaning.

Thus it has been with nursery tales, which of all things one might think would be the least likely to throw any light upon the past, or to yield instruction as they yield amusement. For some years learned men have taken down these tales from the lips of old goodies, unlearned peasants, and servants in India, Germany, Russia, Scotland and elsewhere, and on putting them side by side, have traced a strong likeness running through the whole. Now we are sure that the old grannies in Northern Europe did not learn their tales from Hindu books or story-tellers, and the resemblance can be explained only by supposing that the Aryan tribes carried with them from their one Asian home a common stock of stories as well as a common speech and a common name for the Heaven-Father.

What was the foundation of all these stories we shall presently see; but it cost great labour to get at, because the older form had become overlaid, the gods of the early myths being the heroes of mock history, and these again the giants and knights of fireside tales.

The question was asked if the mythologies of

the ancients were merely absurd stories invented to please a low, bad taste, or stories which held within them a pure meaning, hidden, but not departed ? For if this better meaning could be found it might tell something of the purpose myths once served to those who framed them, and of the views they had of things.

In looking at the Greek myths, it seemed unlikely that a people who have made the world more beautiful to all of us, whose sweet singers charm us still, and of whose wise teachers the wisest of our time gladly learn, should have been the sons of men who invented out of filthy minds the mass of coarse and horrid stories which make up so much of their mythology; such as those telling of Kronos maiming his father and swallowing his own children; of Tantalus roasting his son and giving the gods his flesh to eat; and of Œdipus killing his father and becoming the husband of his own mother.

The doubt led, as doubts always lead, to enquiry, and the enquiry brought out the truth that the older meaning of these tales had been forgotten by the later Greeks, the wisest among whom were shocked at such stories of the gods, one of them saying, 'If the gods do aught unseemly, then they are not gods at all.'

They could not trace, as we can, their birthplace, their language, and their legends to the old Aryan home, and accounted for these things in a proud and foolish way. They called every people around them *barbarians,* in mockery of the *barbar* of which their language seemed made up.

The mode by which the meaning of the Greek myths has been found is this: The earliest forms of myth are contained in the Veda; and the older Sanskrit, in which it is written, has preserved the first forms of the words more than the later Sanskrit or any other Aryan language. Therefore Greek words, the meaning of which was wholly or partly hidden, but the kindred forms of which in Sanskrit were known, were compared with them, and then the meaning became clear. For example, in Greek legend, Athênê is said to be the daughter of Zeus, having sprung from his forehead.

Taking this by itself, its meaning is hard to find. But when, as we saw at page 88, the Greek *Zeus* is found to be the Sanskrit *Dyaus*, we know that something about the *sky* is meant. The Greek *Athênê* is probably the Sanskrit *Ahanâ*, which means the *dawn*. A hymn in the Veda says of her: 'Ahanâ comes near to every house, she who makes every day to be known.' Therefore the Greek legend may be said to mean that the dawn springs from the forehead of the sky, or, as we should say in English, rises out of the east.

Now, although such a myth as that of Athênê, with very many others that could be told, are to us but sweet and pretty conceits, they were not so to the Aryans, who, as we have seen, believed all things which moved to have life; sun, moon, star, and uprising, fleet-footed dawn a strong, grand life, and who spoke of them accordingly, meaning what they said, and not composing poetry for men to admire. Language is not the only proof of this; for the accounts which travellers give concerning the nature-myths framed by modern savages, in which dead but moving things are called living persons, show that the mind of man worked then as it works now. And the notions which young children often form about their toys aptly illustrate the mythic age through which every race passes. 'To a little child not only are all living creatures endowed with human intelligence, but everything is alive. In his world pussy takes rank with Pa and Ma in point of intelligence. He beats the chair against which he has knocked his head; the fire that burns his finger is "naughty fire;" and the stars that shine through his bedroom-window are eyes, like mamma's or pussy's, only brighter.'

And it is the same with man in a rude, untaught state, nor does he reach loftier ideas till a long time after his civilization has begun.

How true all this is we can never deeply feel, because it is not possible for us to put ourselves in the place of man in the myth-making stage of his growth. If we could forget all that science has taught us and believe that the sun was alive, we too, as the dreadful night wore away and the light of the stars grew fainter, should look with blended hope and fear to the east, and then, seeing the light-rays creeping up followed by the sun, welcome him as our life and say of him many things, calling him eye of heaven, a face with streaming locks, a god drawn by brilliant horses, a golden bird that died in the flame and rose again from the ashes. We too should speak of him as loving the dawn (an idea which has given rise to many tender myths), and when he sank in the west, and the soft light floated over him, as soothed to sleep or to death by the kisses of his loved one.

A careful study of the Aryan myths shows that they had for the larger part their birth in the ideas called forth by the changing scenery of the heavens in dawn and dusk, in sunrise and sunset, and the myriad shades and fleeting forms which lie between them; the dawn being the source of the richest myths. Of course every myth and legend is not to be thus accounted for, because that which is human and personal takes shape and substance likewise. The mood of mind caused by things sad or joyful in the life of man; the sense of right and wrong, and the knowledge that within us the battle between these two is being fought; these, which are to those who feel deeply more real than even sunrises and sunsets, have had a large share in adding to the legends which make us creep closer to the light and move us now to laughter and now to tears. Then many events of history have been so misunderstood as to become mythical. Fable has been promoted into history; history has been lowered into fable; and history and fable have become mixed and gathered round great names, such as Cyrus, Charlemagne and far greater names than theirs.

Prof. Max Müller shows how easily a myth might grow out of the word *gloaming* (or evening twilight). Supposing that the exact meaning had been forgotten and that a proverb had been preserved in this form, 'The gloaming sings the sun to sleep,' an explanation would be needed. Nurses would tell their children that the gloaming was a good old woman who came every night to put the sun into his bed and who would be very angry if she found any little children still awake. The children would soon talk among themselves about Nurse Gloaming, and as they grew up would tell their children again of the same wonderful old nurse. It was in this and similar ways that in the childhood of the world many a story grew up which, adapted and decorated by a poet, became part and parcel of what we call the mythology of ancient nations.

I must now tell you about one very important Aryan myth which has given rise to a group of legends, and even become part of some great religions. All the Aryan nations, and also some other nations with whom they have had intercourse, have among their legends the story of a battle between a hero and a monster. In each case the hero is the victor and sets free treasures which have been stolen and hidden by the monster, and so renders help to men. In Hindu myth it is the combat between Indra and the dragon Vritra; among the Romans it became the fight between Hercules and the three-headed monster Cacus; with the Greeks, among other like tales, it was the battle between Apollo and the terrible snake Pythôn; in old Norse legend, between Sigurd and the coiled dragon Fafnir; and in Christian myth between St George and the Dragon. We shall see what grave form the battle took in the old Persian religion and how the Satan of later Jewish belief was borrowed therefrom.

Let us now trace the birth and growth of this myth. Since the chief wealth of the Aryans was in their cattle, each man would do his utmost to increase the number of his flocks and herds. The cow was the creature most prized, for her milk fed his household and every calf that was born made him richer. She was to him what the camel is to the Arab and the buffalo to the Red Indian. And as she was the sign of fruitfulness and welcome gifts, so the bull was the sign of strength. The Aryan's enemy was he who stole the cattle, while he who saved them from the robber's clutch was the true friend.

We have seen where the Aryan looked for the dwelling-place of his gods. As he, in whom was born that same sense of wonder which his savage forefathers had, and which we his children have, lifted his eyes to the heaven whose rains watered the ground he tilled and whose sun ripened his fruits, he saw the clouds moving in their great majesty, filled through and through with the light or hiding it within their dark caverns. Nothing strikes man everywhere so much as the struggle between light and darkness; between the lightning piercing the clouds and letting loose the rain and the slow march of the black powers that hold the rain within their grasp; between the sun's rays and the cloud or fog they strive to rend asunder.

The heaven was to the Aryan a great plain over which roamed bulls and cows, for such the clouds seemed to him to be. Just as the cow yielded him milk, so those cows of heaven dropped upon the earth rain and dew, heaven's milk. The lord of the plain was the sun, he was the strong bull of heaven. Nor were these the only animals that wandered across the wide fields above, for endless as are the forms and shades of colour of the clouds so endless were the creatures they were thought to be. The fancy of the myth-maker worked with the freedom with which we in sitting before a fire may picture any number of queer shapes and faces in the red-hot coals.

The Aryan thought that the dark clouds in the sky were the dwelling-place of a wicked monster who had stolen the cows and shut them up in the caverns of the piled-up mountains (the Sanskrit word *parvata* means both *cloud* and *mountain*) and who was drinking up the water needed by the thirsty earth and hiding the treasures of light and heat from men.

Unless the lord of the plains, the bull of bulls, killed this huge black thief (called by different names in the Veda; Vritra, serpent, wolf, black one, &c.), the cows could not be freed and brought back to their pasture. So with the storm-gods riding at his side, Indra (the name given him in the Veda) comes bellowing, the fire (that is, the sun rays or lightning) flashing from him, his horns (or thunderbolts) tossing in anger. He slays the monster, cleaves the rocks asunder, and forthwith the light breaks out or the pent waters are loosed and pour down upon the parched land.

Thus I hope is made clear to you from whence the legends of fights between heroes and monsters have come. It is the victory of light over darkness, but the battle took a more serious shape than that in later ages. The struggle that man saw between the powers of nature was but child's play compared to the deadly conflict between the powers of good and evil as they fought for the mastery over all things; but more of this when we have done with the myths.

The tales of princesses and ladies kept in dark prisons, from which some bold and gallant knight frees them, are later forms of the myths of the sun released from the darkness of the night; of the spring escaped from the chains in which winter had bound him; and of the waters delivered from their cloud-prisons.

This book is only a key to unlock the door to a gallery of wonders where you will find more learned and sure guides than he who now points the way. A mere list of what is to be seen therein would fill a very large book, and I must be content to end this chapter with a few proofs of the pure meaning hidden in Greek and other myths and of some curious likenesses between certain historic tales and nursery legends of East and West.

1. It is said of Kronos (which is a Greek name only) who was a son of Ouranos, with whom the race of gods began, that he swallowed his first five children soon after the birth of each.

Kronos means *time* and Ouranos *the heaven*.

Ouranos is the same as the sky-god *Varuna* invoked in the Veda, whose name comes from a root *var, to veil,* heaven being spread like a veil over the earth.

The Greek myth simply means that Time swallows up the days which spring from it. The German story of the Wolf and the Seven Kids is something like it. 'The wolf swallowed all the kids except the youngest, which was hidden in the clock-case, the meaning being that Night swallows up the days of the week, but cannot eat the youngest because it is hidden, as to-day is, in the clock-case.'

Tantalus (from which comes our word *tantalise,* to torment) was said to be king of Lydia, and when Zeus and all the gods came down to a feast which he gave them, he killed his own son and set the roasted flesh before them, to see whether they knew all things that take place. They knew what he had done and brought back the child to life, sending Tantalus to Tartarus, where all are banished who sin against the gods. There he was made to stand up to his chin in water, which sank lower whenever he tried to drink it;

while branches of fruit hung over his head, but waved away each time that he sought to grasp them. The meaning is that the fierce sun kills the fruits of the earth, while the punishment means that if he glares too fiercely the water courses flee from him and the fruits wither away.

Saranyû is one of the names in Sanskrit for the *dawn*, and it explains the name *Erinyes* given to the Greek furies or avenging gods. For as the morning brings to light the evil deeds done in the darkness, so the *Erinyes*, winged monsters with serpent locks and eyes with tears of blood, found out, and then punished, the crimes of men.

Among the many names for the sun in the Veda, he is called the golden-handed, from the golden rays shooting like fingers from him. In the course of time a story grew up that at a sacrifice he had cut off his hand and that the priests made a golden one in its stead. He was also called a frog when at rising or setting he seemed to be squatting on the water. Now in one of the West Highland tales there is a story of a frog who wishes to marry a princess, and who, when the princess consents to become his wife, is changed into a handsome man. The old meaning of this tale comes out in a Sanskrit story of Bhekî the frog. She was a beautiful girl and one day when sitting near a well, a king saw her and asked her to be his wife. She consented on his promising never to show her a drop of water. One day being faint she asked the king for water; the king forgot his promise, brought her water and she vanished. Both stories grew out of a saying about the sun, such as that Bhekî the sun will die at the sight of water, as we should say that the sun will set when it approaches the water from which it rose in the morning.

From these few examples you will more easily learn how the uncouth features of mythology have been caused by the Aryan tribes, when they became scattered, forgetting the first meaning of the words which they used when together. In looking at the Greek, Norse, German and other myths by the light of the Veda, we find the full, fresh thoughts of the mind of man when there was no bounds to his beliefs and fancies. Nature was the great storehouse from which he drew; the sunlight; the fresh morning air; the floating clouds, wind-driven; the spear-tipped lightning and the heaven-sent rain.

2. And now, as showing how these myths have actually forced their way into history and passed without question for a long time, just as bad coins will now and then pass among good ones, let me say a few words about William Tell.

The story is well known how in the 1307th year after Christ the cruel Gessler set a hat upon a pole as a symbol of the ruling power, and ordered everyone who passed by to bow before it. A mountaineer named Tell refused to obey the order and was at once brought before Gessler. As Tell was known to be an expert archer, he was sentenced by way of punishment to shoot an apple off the head of his own son. The apple was placed on the boy's head and the father bent his bow; the arrow sped and went through the apple. Gessler saw that Tell before shooting had stuck another arrow in his belt and asked the reason. Tell replied: 'To shoot you, tyrant, had I slain my child.' Now although the crossbow which Tell is said to have used is shown at Zurich, the event never took place! One poor man was condemned to be burnt alive for daring to question the story, but the poor man was right. The story is told not only in Iceland, Denmark, Norway, Finland, Russia, Persia, and perhaps India, but is common to the Turks and Mongolians, 'while a legend of the wild Samoyedes, who never heard of Tell or saw a book in their lives, relates it, chapter and verse, of one of their marksmen.' In its English form it occurs in the ballad of William of Cloudeslee. The bold archer says:

> 'I have a sonne seven years old;
> Hee is to me full deere;
> I will tye him to a stake—
> All shall see him that bee here—
> And lay an apple upon his head,
> And goe six paces him froe,
> And I myself with a broad arrowe
> Shall cleave the apple in towe.'

The story is an old Aryan sun-myth. Tell is the sun-god whose arrows (light-rays) never miss their mark, and likewise kill their foes.

There is another old tale over which I have cried as a boy. You have heard how the faithful dog Gellert killed the wolf which had come to destroy Llewellyn's child, and how, when the prince came home, and found the cradle empty, and the dog's mouth smeared with blood, he quickly slew the brave creature, and then found the child safe, and the wolf dead beside it. At Beddgelert in North Wales, you may see the dog's grave neatly railed round!

Now this story occurs in all sorts of forms in the folk-lore of nearly every Aryan people, and is found in China and Egypt. In India a black snake takes the place of the wolf, and the ichneumon that of the dog, while in Egypt the story says that a cook nearly killed a Wali for smashing a pot full of herbs, and then discovered that amongst the herbs there lurked a poisonous snake.

It is safe to conclude that marvellous things which are said to have happened in so many places never happened anywhere.

But if we must give up these stories as legends, it is not all loss, since it tends to bring the story-tellers closer together, and to show how, under different skins, the same hearts are beating, and how the same welcome is given in every age to the tales of brave, of loving, and of faithful deeds which men and women have wrought in this world of ours, and which make the legends possible.

3. But I must forbear, because I am sure you will like to hear a little about some tales that have sometimes dried your tears, and sometimes made you cry.

Let us see whether Cinderella is a British-born lady in disguise, or whether she came from some very old nursery in the East. She must have come therefrom, for we find the framework of the story in the Veda, where Cinderella is a *dawn-maiden!*

The aurora in her flight leaves no footsteps behind her, but the prince Mitra (one of the Vedic names for the sun), while following the beautiful young girl, finds a slipper which shows her footstep and the size of her foot, so small that no other woman has a foot like it. This sun-myth which tells of a lost slipper, and of a prince who tries to find the foot to which it belongs, and who cannot overtake the chariot in which the maiden rides, is the source of the dear old tale. Cinderella, as you will remember, was beautiful only when in the ball-room, or near the shining light. This means that the aurora is bright only when the sun is near, when he is away, her dress is of sombre colour—she is a *Cinder*ella. The Greek form of the tale says that whilst Rhodopê was bathing, an eagle snatched one of her slippers from her maid and carried it to the King of Egypt, as he sat on his judgment seat at Memphis. The king fell in love with the foot to which the slipper belonged, and gave orders that its owner should be searched for, and when Rhodopê was found, the king married her.

In the Hindu tale a Rajah has an only daughter who was born with a golden necklace which contained her soul, and the father was warned that if the necklace were taken off and worn by another, the princess would die. One birthday he gave her a pair of golden and jewelled slippers which she wore whenever she went out; and one day, as she was picking flowers upon a mountain, a slipper came off and fell down the steep side into the forest below. It was searched for in vain; but not long after, a prince who was hunting found it and took it to his mother, who, judging how fair and highborn the owner must be, advised him to seek for her and make her his wife. He made public the finding of the slipper throughout the kingdom, but no one claimed it, and he had wellnigh despaired when some travellers from the Rajah's country heard that the missing slipper was in the hands of the prince, to whom they made known its owner's name. He straightway repaired to the Rajah's palace, and showing him the slipper, asked for the hand of the princess, who became his wife. After her marriage a jealous woman stole the necklace while she was sleeping, and, to her husband's deep grief, her body was carried to a tomb. But it did not decay, nor did the bloom of life leave her sweet face, so that the prince was glad to visit her tomb; and one day the secret whereby her soul could be restored was revealed to him. He recovered the necklace, placed it round her neck, and with joy brought her back to his palace.

The like framework of a slipper for whose pretty wearer a search is made and who becomes the finder's wife, occurs in the Serbian tale of 'Papalluga;' in the German tale of 'Aschenputtel;' in the fable of La Fontaine about the 'Milkmaid and her Pail;' and other variants of the story, whose birthplace, as we have seen, was in Central Asia. 'Beauty and the Beast' is also found in Hindu, Greek, Norse and other myth.

In the Greek story, Psychê is married to Cupid, who carries her to a secluded garden, where she sees him at night only. Her jealous sisters tell her that she is wedded to a loathly monster; and wishful to know the truth, she draws near to him with a lamp and finds him the loveliest of the gods. But a drop of hot oil fell on him, and he awoke to blame her and vanish. After hard toil and weary search she found him, and was re-united to him for ever. In the German tale, the youngest of three daughters is married to a prince who is a hideous lion by day, and who tells her that he must never see the light. One day a sun-ray falls upon him through the chink of a door, and he is at once changed into a dove and flies away. His bride seeks him, and, aided by the sun, the moon and the north wind, frees him from the spell he is under, and lives with him 'happily ever after.' In the Gaelic tale the husband is a dog in the daytime; while in the Hindu tale it is a princess who is disguised in the skin of a withered old woman, which she takes off before dawn, but puts on again before the day breaks.

In all these there are common features, varied in detail by the story-teller's art and by the nature of the country and people where each has found a home.

Stories collected from very distant parts abound in which the place where some giant or magician keeps his 'soul' or 'heart' or 'strength' is found out by the wily arts of a woman, who thereby has revenge for evil done to her or to her family. In the Norse tale of the 'Giant who had no Heart in his Body,' the monster has turned six princes with their wives into stone, whereupon the seventh brother seeks to take vengeance on him. On his way he succours a raven, a salmon and a wolf, for which kind act each creature renders him service. The wolf carries him to the giant's castle, where the seventh princess is confined, who promises to find out where the giant keeps his heart. He more than once refuses to tell her, or tells her falsely, but at last yields, as Samson yielded to Delilah. He says, 'Far, far away in a lake lies an island; on that island stands a church; in that church is a well; in that well swims a duck; in that duck there is an egg; and in that egg there lies my heart, you darling.' The princess tells this to the prince, who 'rides on the wolf's back to the island; the raven flies to the top of the steeple and gets the church-keys; the salmon dives to the bottom of the well and brings up the egg from the place where the duck had dropped it.' As soon as the prince has the egg, he squeezes it, when the giant begs for his life, which the prince promises, on condition that he brings back to life the six brothers and their wives. But as soon as this is done, the prince breaks his word, squeezes the egg in two, and the giant dies.

The Hindu tale of 'Punchkin' is very like this. A magician turns into stone all the daughters of a Rajah, with their husbands, but saves the youngest daughter, whom he wishes to marry. She has left a son at home, who goes in search of his mother; and finding her in the magician's tower, persuades her to discover the secret place where the tyrant keeps his heart. The ogre tells her that in the middle of the jungle there is a circle of palm-trees, and in the centre of the circle six jars full of water, below which is a little parrot in a cage; and if the parrot is killed, he too will die. The prince goes to the place, which is kept by dragons; but an eagle whom he has helped carries him to the water-jars, which he upsets, and then seizes the parrot. He frightens the magician into restoring his victims to life, and then pulls the bird to pieces. 'As the wings and legs come away, so tumble off the arms and legs of the magician; and finally, as the prince wrings the bird's neck, Punchkin twists his own head round and dies.' In the Arabian story, 'the Jinn's soul is enclosed in the body of a sparrow, which is imprisoned in a box placed in other boxes put in chests contained in a marble coffer, which is sunk in the ocean that surrounds the world.' The coffer is raised by the aid of a seal-ring, the sparrow is taken out and strangled, whereupon the Jinn's body becomes a heap of ashes and the hero escapes with the maiden.

Space quite forbids my quoting more tales of the same kind, which are found in Bohemian, Gaelic, Serbian, and other folk-lore, not forgetting, what is more remarkable than all, that like features exist in an Egyptian tale which is more than three thousand years old.

In the Játaka, a very ancient collection of Buddhist fables which, professing to have been told by Buddha, narrate his exploits in the 550 births through which he passed before attaining Buddhahood, there are found 'not a few of the tales which pass under the name of "Æsop's Fables,"' and of the stories which are like those in other Western folk-lore.

In one of these a holy man, who has attained to a seat in the world of spirits, aids a sick brother by the gift of a magic hatchet, which at bidding brings fuel and makes a fire, and of a magic bowl, whose contents when emptied fill a mighty river; which reminds us of the magic tools in Norse tales; the scissors that cut out silk and satin from the air; the axe that cut the oak which grew bigger at the stroke of every other axe; and the magic salt wherewith the prince, when he frees the princess, makes a great mountain between them and the giant who pursues them. In the Buddhist fables of the ungrateful beast from whose throat the crane removes a bone that stuck there; and of the frightened ass who, clothed in a lion's skin, brays like an ass, we are surprised to find ourselves face to face with familiar tales, part of a vast stock which come to us from far Japan to bleak Iceland, comprising the beast-fables of the world.

In Æsop we read of the fox who will not go into the lion's den, because he sees only the imprint of feet going *in*. In a Hottentot tale it is said that the lion was ill, and that all the beasts went to visit him except the jackal, who would not go, because the footsteps of those who went to see the lion did not turn back. So in a version of the famous old tale of 'Reynard the Fox,' the cock gets his head out of Reynard's mouth by making him answer the farmer; while in the Hottentot tale, the cock makes the jackal say his prayers, and when the befooled beast folds his hands and shuts his eyes, the clever bird flies away.

Then there are other legends and tales which,

like the myths, are born of man's wondering outlook on nature, such as Little Red Riding Hood, who in the German story is cut out of the sleeping wolf by a hunter; Tom Thumb, who was swallowed by the cow, and came out unhurt; Saktidern, swallowed by the fish and cut out again; Jonah, swallowed by a sea-monster which casts him ashore unharmed; all of which are legends telling of the night devouring the sun.

But enough of illustration has been given to show how like to one another are many of the fairy tales, legends and myths of the Indo-European races,* and I must end this long chapter with a brief account of the source from whence have come the stories of the 'House that Jack built,' and of the 'Old Woman who couldn't get her Pig over the Stile.' There is a poem at the end of the book of Passover services used by the Jews, which some among them regard as a parable of the past and future of the Holy Land. It contains ten verses, each ending with the refrain, 'a kid, a kid,' and it begins

'A kid, a kid my father bought
For two pieces of money;'

---

* See Note E.

and after telling how a cat came and ate the kid, and a dog came and bit the cat, and a staff came and beat the dog, and so on, it concludes thus:

> 'Then came the Holy One, blessed be He!
> And killed the Angel of Death,
> That killed the butcher,
> That slew the ox,
> That drank the water,
> That quenched the fire,
> That burned the staff,
> That beat the dog,
> That bit the cat,
> That ate the kid
> That my father bought
> For two pieces of money:
>   A kid, a kid.'

We now bid farewell to the myths and reach a place where the ground is firmer beneath us, where the sky is as full of theme for wonder as it was to the old Aryans. We do not see in the sun a slayer of dragons or a weary traveller; in the lightning a fiery serpent; in the clouds cows with swelling udders to be milked by the wind-god; we see above us the stately, well-ordered march of sun, moon, star and cloud at the command of Him who 'bringeth out their host by number; He calleth them all by names by the greatness of His might, for that He is strong in power,' and we know that 'these are parts of His ways; but how little a portion is heard of Him! the thunder of His power who can understand?'

(f.) THE SEPARATION OF THE ARYAN TRIBES.

At last the time arrived when the mother-country had become too narrow for the growing numbers or when envious hordes burst in upon them, and when some of the children had to leave in search of food and work elsewhere.

It was an eventful period when they set forth to clear a path through the forests and ford the rivers and fight the foes that lay between them and the glorious future into which they were entering. They bore weapons upon their shoulders, but the mightiest weapon which they carried was unseen, even the power which made them men, and through which they or their children would awaken and use the great forces that had long laid safe in Nature's keeping, and also give to the lands over which they spread themselves religion, law and liberty, science, art and song.

There is a noble and stirring description in Charles Kingsley's 'Alton Locke' of the departure of a tribe from its old home, which may fitly be quoted here. He speaks of the 'tall, bare-limbed men, with stone axes on their shoulders and horn bows at their backs;' 'herds of gray cattle, guarded by huge lop-eared mastiffs;' 'shaggy white horses, heavy-horned sheep, and silky goats,' and tells of the path they took: 'Westward, through the boundless steppes, whither or why we knew not; but that the All-Father had sent us forth. And behind us the rosy snow-peaks died into ghastly gray, lower and lower, as every evening came; and before us the plains spread infinite, with gleaming salt-lakes, and ever fresh tribes of gaudy flowers. Behind us dark lines of living beings streamed down the mountain slopes; around us dark lines crawled along the plains—all westward, westward ever. . . . Westward ever, who could stand against us? We met the wild asses on the steppe, and tamed them, and made them our slaves. We slew the bison herds, and swam broad rivers on their skins. The Python snake lay across our path; the wolves and wild dogs snarled at us out of their coverts; we slew them and went on. The forest rose in black tangled barriers; we hewed our way through them and went on. Strange giant tribes met us, and eagle-visaged hordes, fierce and foolish; we smote them hip and thigh, and went on, westward ever.'

If you look at a map of Asia you will see that the country where the eastern tribes dwelt is hemmed in by lofty mountains, while the region where the other tribes dwelt lies open to the west. Since those to the east could not enlarge their borders in that quarter, they pushed the others towards the land that stretched between them and Europe, which caused the Celtic tribes, who lived most to the west and whose descendants are found in the most westerly parts of Europe, to be the first to leave. These pioneers slowly overspread the face of Europe, and traces of the paths which they took remain in the Celtic names of places where they settled, and especially of rivers on whose banks they dwelt. They have ever been a restless people, but had they been disposed to settle they would have found it no easy task. The races who were already in possession of the soil did not yield without a struggle, while long afterwards there poured in from the east the other Aryan emigrants to Europe. So the Celts had at last a hard time of it, and were driven onwards by the Germans and Slavonians, who seem to have travelled by a path north of the Caspian Sea, and by the common forefathers of the Greeks and Romans, who took a more southerly road, which brought them to the lands made famous by their sons.

Thus the old home was slowly cleared of most of its former inmates, and those who stayed behind, the ancestors of the Medes and Persians and Hindus, found wider breathing space, and came down from the higher valleys in the east to the more fertile parts.

Thus is explained the movements of the two branches of the Aryan family of mankind.

With this brief account we must now take leave of the tribes that went to Europe and follow the fortunes of those who remained together for a time. Their separation will lead me to speak of the growth of Hinduism or Brahmanism out of the old Aryan faith ; of the rise of Zoroastrianism, the ancient religion of Persia; and of Buddhism.

After an account of these three great Aryan religions, we will cast a brief glance at the religions of China and then say somewhat of the Semitic race, among whom Judaism and Mohammadanism had their birth.

We shall thus have taken a rough survey of most of the living religions of the world, and I hope gained some clearer knowledge of the beliefs of hundreds of millions of our fellow-creatures.

LANGUAGE, the same witness of which so large a use has been made already, is called in to prove that the Eastern Aryans dwelt together for some time, united by nearly the same speech, by worship of the same gods, and observance of the same rites of their old religion. There are, however, traditions of a state of turmoil and of struggles with the restless tribes around them, who doubtless coveted the richer land where the Aryans had settled; still more of quarrels among themselves which gave rise to bitter hatred and then to separation, one branch moving southwards into India. In the Zend-Avesta clear mention is made of this dispute, and although we do not know all the causes which led thereto, we know that religion had much, perhaps most, to do with it.

We saw that the old Aryan faith was an almost pure nature-religion, a worship of the powers which were seen in action around. Out of this there was slowly growing, as the result of man's thought about things and comparison of them with one another, a sense that underneath the *many* there was the *one*, and thus he was being led to the highest of all beliefs, that 'there is one God and none other but He.'

Among the men whom God sends but rarely, charged with this message of His unity, none stand out in purer outline than Zarathustra (commonly spelt, according to the Greek, Zoroaster). To him was given the great work of reforming, as he said, the faith of his country, and of founding a religion which was the grandest of all the Aryan creeds.

He met with bitter opposition from those who clung to the older and grosser faith, but these were worsted in the struggle; and at last the separation was complete. The tribes who would not accept the new religion had, there is reason for thinking, already crossed the passes of the high mountain-range named the Hindu Kush, and after settling in the Punjab, slowly pushed their way along the valley of the Ganges, spreading themselves in the course of centuries over India.

India is a land of mixed races. There are found among her tangled forests and rugged hills remnants of a savage people whose forefathers were probably the earliest dwellers, makers of the rough stone weapons found in various parts. These were subdued by invaders from the north-west, who were of a race allied to the Finns, Lapps, Mongols, &c., a race which seems to have covered large tracts of country, and to have laid the foundation upon which both the Aryan and Semitic families built their higher culture. They were far above the wild creatures whom they displaced and therefore no mean foes for the Aryans to meet. The many huge erections of stones, in the form of circles, tables, &c., which India contains and which are older than the rock-cut temples of the Buddhists, are their handiwork. But they had to yield before the greater force and skill of the Aryans, and when caste was established, to take their place in the lowest class; their language, religion and customs being more or less altered.

Up to the time of the entrance of the Aryans into India scarcely a date is at hand to help us, neither does history become much clearer afterwards, since the Hindus have been strangely careless in such a matter; unlike the Egyptians, who put down the time when the smallest events of daily life took place.

We will now pass on to some account of the Vedic faith and the religion which sprang therefrom.

CHAPTER VII.

THE ANCIENT AND MODERN HINDU RELIGIONS.

THE religion known as Brahmanism or Hinduism includes at this day the many Hindu sects who differ very much from one another, each having its own form of belief and worship, but all revering the Vedas as the inspired word of God, and numbering together about 120 millions of mankind, or one-tenth of the human race. Some, however, state their number at 150 millions. Unlike the religions founded by Christ, Zoroaster, and Mohammad, the history of Brahmanism does not gather round a person. A lifetime would not compass the study of its sacred books, and it is a religion very hard to explain, indeed we know far less about it than we know about the old Aryan religion of which it is the corrupt offspring. It is like a mass of shapely and shapeless things huddled together, which no manner of art could arrange into a well-set whole. It is rich with the profoundest and the saddest thought of a deeply religious people, but teaching that it should be the end of every life to shut its ears to the call of duty, to be unmoved by pleasure or by pain, and to sit down to dreamy thinking, it has caused the Hindus to run into the grossest and most loathsome superstitions, and to obey the most foolish, priest-made rules about food and cleansing and such like things.

This must be the case with every religion which strives to dry up the passions and emotions of men, instead of turning them into channels where they may flow to benefit and bless others.

In tracing the history of Brahmanism, we must begin with some account of the religion of the Aryan Hindus, of which a knowledge is obtained from the Vedas.

The discovery of these ancient scriptures has been an immense gain, for without them we should have remained ignorant of the causes which led to the founding of Zoroastrianism and Buddhism, as well as of the nature of the old Aryan religion and from which the Vedic religion differs but little.

That the narrative may flow on without too many breaks, I have removed to Note F at the end of this book, a list of the names and contents of the Hindu sacred writings, which should be read as a help to understanding this chapter.

Veda means *knowledge, science,* and is a word kindred to our English *wisdom, to wit,* and the many like words. Although it is used in a plural form to include four collections of hymns, there is but one true, ancient Veda, called the *Rig-Veda,* and from that our account of the old Hindu faith will be drawn.

It contains the hymns in which the Aryans who first entered India, praised their gods, and the oldest of such hymns are believed to have been composed 2400 years before Christ, or above 4200 years ago. They exceed 1000 in number, and are of various lengths, from one to more than fifty verses or *ric,* meaning *praise,* hence the name *Rig-Veda,* or *Veda of praise.* Their authors are called *Rishis,* which means *seer* or *sage.*

Some 600 years before Christ every word, every verse and every syllable was counted, and the number agrees with existing copies as nearly as one could expect. The Brahmans have the holiest veneration for the four Vedas, and believe them to be so entirely the work of God as to have existed in His mind before time began. They make a great difference between these writings and all the others, which they call *Smriti*, or *tradition*, or that which is handed down from ancient teachers by one age after another; while the Vedas and Brâhmanas are *Sruti*, or *hearing*, *revelation*, or that which comes direct from God.

The gods chiefly addressed in the Rig-Veda are Agni, fire; Prithivî, the earth; Maruts, the storm; Ushas, &c., the dawn; Mitra, Sûrya, &c., the sun; Varuna, the all-surrounder; Indra, the sky; and Soma, a name given at a later period to the moon. Vishnu, who afterwards became a leading god in the Hindu Trimûrti, or Trinity, is also a name for the sun in the Veda.

As stated at page 87, the Aryan did not place the earth in the highest rank; she was only partly divine. It was not so, however, with fire, that thing of mystery and shapeless power, a merciless master, a helpful servant, at whose worship none can be amazed. Agni, god of fire (akin to Latin *ignis*, whence our word *ignite*, to *set on fire*), has more hymns addressed to him than any other god. He it is who lives among men, who is the messenger between earth and heaven, the sole guarding and guiding power left to shelter men and dispel the gloom when the sun has set. His wonderful birth from two pieces of wood rubbed together is sung in glowing language, the ten fingers of the kindler are ten virgins who bring him into being; the two pieces of wood are his father and mother. Because the butter when thrown into the flame makes it mount higher and burn brighter, it was believed to be the gift Agni loved best, and as the flame rose upwards it was believed to carry to heaven the gifts heaped upon it. This is one of many hymns to him:

'Agni, accept this log which I offer to thee, accept this my service; listen well to these my songs.

'With this log, O Agni, may we worship thee, thou son of strength, conqueror of horses! and with this hymn, thou high-born!

'May we thy servants serve thee with songs, O granter of riches, thou who lovest songs and delightest in riches.

'Thou lord of wealth and giver of wealth, be thou wise and powerful; drive away from us the enemies!

'He gives us rain from heaven, he gives us inviolable strength, he gives us food a thousandfold.

'Youngest of the gods, their messenger, their invoker, most deserving of worship, come, at our praise, to him who worships thee and longs for thy help.

'For thou, O sage, goest wisely between these two creations (heaven and earth, gods and men), like a friendly messenger between two hamlets.

'Thou art wise, and thou hast been pleased; perform thou, intelligent Agni, the sacrifice without interruption, sit down on this sacred grass!'

In our account of the religion of Zoroaster, we shall see what awe his followers felt towards fire, as the nearest emblem of the divine.

Among the gods of the air, we find hymns in the Veda to the Maruts and others, but it is Indra who receives highest praise. Dyaus, as we have already seen, was one of the names common among the undivided Aryans, but among the Hindu tribes his place was taken by Indra. Indra rose from Dyaus, the sky, who was his father, and from Prithivî, the earth, where she and sky met, therefore Prithivî was his mother. This Vedic myth of Indra as their son is kept in mind at Brahman marriages, when the bridegroom says to the bride, 'I am the sky, thou art the earth, come let us marry.' It is Indra, you will remember, who slays the demon Vritra, and who is refreshed for his mighty deed by drinking three lakes of *soma*, the water of strength.

Soma (see p. 94) means 'extract,' and the plant from which it is obtained is akin to the common milkweed. The Aryans no sooner found out the strange power in the juice to excite and produce frenzy, than they believed it to be divine, since it seemed to give a godlike strength. It was raised to the rank of a god, and called king of heaven and earth, conqueror of all. The hymns to Soma occupy an entire book of the Veda: one of the most beautiful is quoted at page 111 of the 'Childhood of the World,' and therefore need not be repeated here.

Indra is praised thus in the Rig-Veda:

'He who as soon as born is the first of the deities, who has done honour to the gods by his deeds; he at whose might heaven and earth are alarmed and who is known by the greatness of his strength; he, men, is Indra.

'He who fixed firm the moving earth, who spread the spacious firmament; he, men, is Indra.

'He who having destroyed Vritra, set free the seven rivers:

who recovered the cows; who generated fire in the clouds; who is invincible in battle; he, men, is Indra.

'He to whom heaven and earth bow down; he at whose might the mountains are appalled; he who is drinker of the Soma juice, the firm of frame, the adamant armed, the wielder of the thunderbolt; he, men, is Indra. May we envelope thee with acceptable praises as husbands are embraced by their wives.'

Among the gods that bring the light, Ushas, the dawn, calls forth the richest songs, for she it is who chases the darkness and makes ready a pathway for the sun, and who awakens in every Brahman's breast the morning prayer which for full four thousand years has gone up from pious Hindus: 'Let us meditate on the adorable light of the divine creator; may He rouse our minds!'

Here is a fine, simple hymn to Ushas:

'She shines upon us, like a young wife, rousing every living being to go to his work. When the fire had to be kindled by men, she made the light by striking down darkness.

'She rose up, spreading far and wide, and moving everywhere. She grew in brightness, wearing her brilliant garment. The mother of the cows (that is, the mornings), the leader of the days, she shone gold-coloured, lovely to behold.

'She, the fortunate, who brings the eye of the gods, who leads the white and lovely steed (of the sun), the dawn was seen revealed by her rays, with brilliant treasures, following every one.

'Thou who art a blessing where thou art near, drive far away the unfriendly; make the pasture wide, give us safety! Scatter the enemy, bring riches! Raise up wealth to the worshipper, thou mighty Dawn.

'Shine for us with our best rays, thou bright Dawn, thou who lengthenest our life, thou the love of all, who givest us food, who givest us wealth in cows, horses and chariots.

'Thou daughter of the sky, thou high-born Dawn, whom the Vasishthas magnify with songs, give us riches high and wide: all ye gods protect us always with your blessings.'

(Vasishtha is the name of one of the chief poets of the Veda.)

After these gladsome words the poet thinks of the many dawns that have come and gone and of the eyes that once saw them and now see them no more, and the thought finds words in a sadder song.

Of the many gods yet remaining, I can only speak of Varuna, noblest and best. For he rules over all; he governs the seasons of the year; he sets sun, moon and stars in their courses, and it is of him that the sin-stricken worshippers ask for pardon and deliverance from evil. For he surrounds them all, and his messengers note down the wrongdoings of men and cast sickness and death upon the wicked. *Amhas*, the Sanskrit word for *sin*, is a very forceful one. It comes from a root meaning to *choke* or *throttle*, for the hold which sin has upon a man is as the grasp of the murderer on the throat of his victim.

Professor Max Müller says that 'the consciousness of sin is a leading feature in the religion of the Veda, so is likewise the belief that the gods are able to take away from man the heavy burden of his sins. And when we read such words as " Varuna is merciful even to him who has committed sin," we should surely not allow the strange name of Varuna to jar on our ears, but should remember that it is but one of the many names which men invented in their helplessness to express their ideas of the Deity.' That Varuna should have appeared to the Hindu as a god to whom sin was hateful and to whom mercy was a delight, proves how nearly he had reached the truth about One who 'is of purer eyes than to behold iniquity.'

Some of the verses in this hymn bear a strong likeness to one of the grandest Psalms in the Bible, the 139th;

'The great lord of these worlds sees as if he were near. If a man thinks he is walking by stealth, the gods know it all.

'If a man stands or walks or hides, if he goes to lie down or to get up, what two people sitting together whisper, King Varuna knows it, he is there as the third.'

(So the Psalmist says: 'Thou compassest my path and my lying down and art acquainted with all my ways.' Verse 3.)

'This earth, too, belongs to Varuna the king, and this wide sky with its ends far apart. The two seas (the sky and the ocean) are Varuna's loins; he is also contained in this drop of water.

'He who should flee far beyond the sky, even he would not be rid of Varuna the king. His spies proceed from heaven towards this world; with thousand eyes they overlook this earth. (Compare with this verses 7 to 12 of the same psalm.)

King Varuna sees all this, what is between heaven and earth, and what is beyond. He has counted the twinklings of the eyes of men. As a player throws the dice, he settles all things.

'May all thy fatal nooses, which stand spread out seven by seven and threefold, catch the man who tells a lie, may they pass by him who tells the truth.'

I must not omit a few verses from prayers in which pardon for sin is sought:

'However we break thy laws from day to day, men as we are, O god Varuna,

'Do not deliver us unto death, nor to the blow of the furious, nor to the wrath of the spiteful!'

Again:

'Wise and mighty are the works of him who stemmed asunder the wide firmaments (heaven and earth). He lifted on high the bright and glorious heaven; he stretched out apart the starry sky and the earth.

'I ask, O Varuna! wishing to know this my sin. I go to ask the wise. The sages all tell me the same: Varuna it is who is angry with thee. . . .

'Absolve us from the sins of our fathers, and from those which we committed with our own bodies.'

The following contains some of the finest verses in the Veda:

'Let me not yet, O Varuna! enter into the house of clay; have mercy, almighty, have mercy!

'If I go along trembling, like a cloud driven by the wind; have mercy, almighty, have mercy!

'Through want of strength, thou strong and bright god, have I gone wrong; have mercy, almighty, have mercy!

'Thirst came upon the worshipper, though he stood in the midst of the waters; have mercy, almighty, have mercy!

'Whenever we men, O Varuna! commit an offence before the heavenly host, whenever we break the law through thoughtlessness; punish us not, O god, for that offence!'

There is plenty of proof in the Veda that the ancient Hindus believed in a life after death.

The king of that other world is Yama. He and his sister Yami are said to have been the first pair, and when they reached the abode of bliss to have made ready a place for those who should follow them. In Persian legend Yama appeared as Yima, ruler of the golden age and founder of Paradise.

Life to these Eastern Aryans was a sunny, joyful thing, and no sad, thought-filled burden. In their prayers they asked for wealth, children, long life, success in war, and yet did not shrink with any needless dread at the fact that life must one day have an end. They believed that in some bright place where the gods dwelt they and their loved ones would be gathered under the peaceful sway of Yama. They made offerings to the spirits of their forefathers as a pious duty, and laid the bodies of their dead in the ground 'in sure and certain hope' that the soul was safe with Yama. At a later date the body was burned on the altar of Agni, that it might ascend through him to the gods and be reunited to the spirit. There is in the Rig-Veda a hymn of surpassing tenderness and beauty, which is still used at Hindu funeral ceremonies. After some verses, in which Death is asked to harm the suppliants no more, the body was placed in the ground with these soft, sweet words:

'Approach thou now the lap of Earth, thy mother,
　　The wide-extending Earth, the ever-kindly;
A maiden soft as wool to him who comes with gifts,
　　She shall protect thee from destruction's bosom.

'Open thyself, O Earth, and press not heavily;
　　Be easy of access and of approach to him,
As mother with her robe her child,
　　So do thou cover him, O earth!

'May Earth maintain herself thus opened wide for him;
　　A thousand props shall give support about him;
And may those mansions ever drip with fatness;
　　May they be there for evermore his refuge.

'Forth from about thee thus I build away the ground;
　　As I lay down this clod may I receive no harm;
This pillar may the Fathers here maintain for thee;
　　May Yama there provide for thee a dwelling.'

Such were the hymns and prayers in which the Vedic worshippers addressed their gods as they smeared the sacred grass with soma-juice or poured butter on the fire. The Veda contains a large number of commonplace and foolish hymns, but we judge the book by what in it is best. The power of writing worthy songs of praise to God is a rare gift; as rare to-day as in that far-off time.

The Vedic religion had no temples, no priesthood, no idols. The millions of gods which are the objects of Hindu worship now, the division of men into castes, the horrid practice (now forbidden) of burning women with their dead husbands, the belief that the soul after death enters the body of one animal after another; formed no part of the old religion, the freshness of which faded away under these and like corrupting forces. That religion, traces of which, mixed with devil and serpent-worship, still linger among the dwellers in remote places, on hills and amidst jungles, was followed by a time when the human mind was stirred by the great questions which lay behind the simple nature-worship; when it asked who knew whence and why all things were? One by one Indra and Agni and the rest fell from their high places to lower ones, and became symbols of the supreme soul Brahmă or Brahm.*

* See note G.

Of the subtle systems which had birth in those times nothing can be said here, and we will deal with the common belief only.

There came to the front a class of men called Brahmans, who have ever since had the highest honour paid them, and who were quick to claim power over others and to build upon the Vedas a huge system by which to rule every moment of a man's life.

In Vedic times, the inhabitants were of two classes; the fair-skinned Aryans and the dark-skinned races whom they had subdued. But the Brahmans pretended that the Veda gave its sanction to a division of the people into castes. It was made to say that when Brahmâ created men, the Brahmans or priests came from his mouth, the soldiers from his arm, the traders and farmers from his thigh, and the Sudras (the conquered race in India) from his foot. The Brahmans thus set themselves over all. They laid down rules so strict about prayers and sacrifices and made the favour of the gods to depend on such trifling things, that every one was glad to secure their help to do these duties aright. The people believed that the Brahmans alone knew what foods might be eaten, what air might be breathed, what clothes might be worn, and what was the proper length of the ladle in which the offering was to be put. No wonder that against so dead a creed and against such claims as these Buddha rose in revolt and founded that great religion which crushed Brahmanism for centuries, and which, although it has scarcely any followers in the land of its birth, is still professed by hundreds of millions of human beings. The chief gods of the later Hindu religion, which has traces of the Buddhism overthrown by it, are Brahmâ, Vishnu and Siva, forming the Hindu Trinity or Trimûrti (from *tri*, three, and *murti*, form). Vishnu and Siva had their different worshippers, which gave rise to two large sects, but the Brahmans, who feared that their power would decay as these sects increased, cleverly united those two gods to Brahmâ, and the pious Hindu bows his head alike to each. In the present day Brahmâ, Vishnu and Siva are worshipped as three in one, their symbol being the sacred word *Om*. The words of an ancient Hindu poet have been thus translated :—

> 'In those Three Persons the One God was shown,
> Each First in place, each Last,—not one alone;
> Of Siva, Vishnu, Brahmâ, each may be
> First, second, third, among the Blessed Three.'

Brahmâ is the Creator, Vishnu the preserver, and Siva the destroyer.

Brahmâ has neither temples nor altars of his own, but images of him are found in the temples of other gods. He is far removed from the worship of men, for as creator of all he remains in calm repose; a motionless majesty, away from the world where life is ever battling with death, and will so remain until the end of present things. He is figured as a four-headed god, bearing in his hands the Vedas, a rosary and vessels for purifying.

Vishnu receives the worship of millions, and has great honour paid him as Krishna, one of the forms in which they believe he came to earth. The *Avatárs* of Vishnu are his descents to this world from time to time to save it when ruin threatened it at the hands of king, giant, or demon, and he then comes under the disguise of man or animal. As such a divine deliverer the brightest memories crowd round him under the myth of Krishna. A mighty demon-king, Kansa, had rule over the world, and when he heard that a child was born who would grow up and destroy him, he ordered a general slaughter of young boys, hoping thus to kill the child. But it was sent to a place of safety and grew up as beautiful Krishna, god of love, and slayer of Kansa. This was the eighth incarnation or avatár of Vishnu, his ninth being, according to some Hindu writings, as the Buddha; and at his tenth and last, he will make an end of all things, and sleeping on the waters that will cover the world when the tortoise that holds it up sinks under his load, will produce Brahmâ, who will create the world anew.

Siva, whose name does not occur in the Vedic hymns, but whose worship prevailed from remote times in India, called forth a different class of worshippers, for fear and terror brought them to his feet. Flood and earthquake, drought and tempest, and worst of all, dark death, were his work. His queen was Kali, terrible black goddess, in whose honour very loathsome things were once done. Siva is figured with a rope for strangling evil-doers, with necklace of human skulls, with earrings of serpents and with the sacred river Ganges upon his head. He is called 'Ganges-bearer,' because when that river descended from heaven he checked the torrent, so that the earth might bear its fall.

Besides these three great gods, there are some of the old Vedic gods who still command reverence, while the lesser gods are to be counted by millions. And we must not forget how large a share of worship has been paid to the bull and cow; a worship which, we can well understand, arose among the undivided Aryans, since it spread into Northern lands, as well as into India. Brahmanism at this day includes the few who believe that nothing exists but spirit, that all else is unreal, that to get united to this spirit and thus freed from the ills of time is the true and only bliss; and the many who go their round of priest-bidden duty month by month; paying worship in June, to the river Ganges, whose sacred waters cleanse from sin and make the low-caste holy; in July, to the famous Jaganâth (Juggernaut); in August, to Krishna, and so on throughout the year; and who expect when they die, not the meeting of friend with friend in the heaven where Yama rules, but an entrance into the body of one animal after another until, made quite pure, their soul is united to the supreme Soul.

This account, meagre as it is, has already run to greater length than I had intended. A full statement of the religions of India; land of dazzling marvels, of many races and many sects, some of them, as the Sikhs and the Jainas, important enough to take rank as separate religions; land upon which Greeks, Mohammadans, English and others have set their greedy eyes; would have to tell of strangely mixed beliefs, some loftiest of any that have dwelt in the mind of man, others lowest to which poor wild savage has clung.

Brahmanism is slowly giving way before the higher teaching of Christians and Mohammadans, and of a few earnest men in its midst who are striving to purify it, and to win the Hindus to the simple creed which underlies the world's great religions and which shows itself in doing and not in dreaming.

We must hope that Christian missionaries will cease to feel jealous when Hindus become Mohammadans, that Mohammadans will cease their bitter hate against Christians, and that each will take pains to understand what the religion of the other is. They will then find how much there is upon which they can agree, and so leave each other free to work for the good of mankind.

CHAPTER VIII.

ZOROASTRIANISM; THE ANCIENT RELIGION OF PERSIA.

OF Zoroaster, the founder of the religion of the Pârsîs (or people of Pârs, that is, ancient Persia,) we have no trustworthy account. There are many Greek, Roman and Persian legends of the miracles which he worked and of the temptations which he overcame, but they throw little or no light upon his true history.

He was probably born in Bactria, and his name implies that he became one of the priests who attended upon the sacred fire. We are sure that he lived more than three thousand years ago, because his religion was founded before the conquest of Bactria by the Assyrians, which took place about twelve hundred years before Christ. It has been argued, chiefly from the strong likeness between Jewish and Persian legends, that he was a neighbour of Abraham, but of this the proof is far too slender.

He was a man of mighty mind; one not content to worship powers that ruled the darkness and the light, but that seemed to have no sway over the heaving sea of human passion and sorrow. To him was given the message of One Who was Lord of all, and Who was not to Zoroaster a being like unto man. He was *Ahura*, 'Spiritual Mighty-One;' *Mazdâ*, 'Creator of All.' *Ahura-Mazdâ* (afterwards corrupted into *Ormuzd*) is thus spoken of in the Zend-Avesta, an account of the contents of which book is given in Note H.

'Blessed is he, blessed are all men to whom the living wise God of his own command should grant those two everlasting powers (immortality and purity). I believe thee, O God, to be the best thing of all, the source of light for the world. Everyone shall choose thee as the source of light, thee, thee, holiest Mazdâ! . . .

'I ask thee, tell me it right, thou living God! Who was from the beginning the Father of the pure world? Who has made a path for the sun and for the stars? Who (but thou) makes the moon to increase and to decrease? This I wish to know, except what I already know.

'Who holds the earth and the skies above it? Who made the waters and the trees of the field? Who is in the winds and storms that they so quickly run? Who is the Creator of the good-minded beings, thou Wise? Who has made the kindly light and the darkness, the kindly sleep, and the awaking!

'Who has made the mornings, the noons and the nights, they who remind the wise of his duty?'

In a later part of the Zend-Avesta, Zoroaster asked Ormuzd what was the most powerful spell to guard against evil. He was answered by the Supreme Spirit that to utter the twenty different names of Ahura-Mazdâ protects best from evil, and thereupon Zoroaster asks what these are. He is told that the first is, 'I am;' the sixth, 'I am wisdom,' and so on until the twentieth, which is 'I am who I am, Mazdao.' Highest of all, Ahura-Mazdâ, was said to have below him angels who did his bidding, 'Immortal Holy Ones,' whose names seem to be echoes of the Vedic gods, and by whose aid good deeds are wrought, and gifts bestowed upon men.

I should say that the feeling between those who clung to the older faith and the followers of Zoroaster grew so bitter that the gods of the Vedic hymns became demons in the Zend-Avesta. In that book Indra is an evil being; in the Vedic belief Ahura is a demon. The Devas of the

Veda are the Daevas or evil spirits of the Zend-Avesta, and the converts to the new religion had to declare that they ceased to worship the Devas. It is well nigh certain that Zoroaster believed in one God, and explained the mystery of evil as the work of demons ruled by an archfiend 'Angra-Mainyus,' the 'Sinful-minded,' afterwards known as Ahriman. In the course of time, as men saw that the powers of good and evil seemed equal, neither being able to conquer, Ahriman was held to be as supreme over evil as Ormuzd was over good. The Supreme mind that had fashioned all was forgotten, and the universe was regarded as a battle-field whereon these two waged unceasing war, not as between Indra and Vritra, for a herd of heavenly cows, but for dominion over all things, Ahriman having, like Ormuzd, ranks of angels who served him.

The thought of evil around him and within him caused Zoroaster to feel heavy at heart, but it did not make him fold his hands in despair. In the Gâthâs or oldest part of the Zend-Avesta, which contains the leading doctrines of Zoroaster, he asks Ormuzd for truth and guidance and desires to know what he shall do. He is told to be pure in thought, word and deed; to be temperate, chaste and truthful; to offer prayer to Ormuzd and the powers that fight with him; to destroy all hurtful things (the ancient Persians looked upon ants, snakes and all vermin, as agents of the evil powers); and to do all that will increase the well-being of mankind. Men were not to cringe before the powers of darkness as slaves crouch before a tyrant, they were to meet them upstanding, and confound them by unending opposition and the power of a holy life.

To such high thoughts, to be sweetened and kept in vigour by pure deeds, did this noble man give utterance, and we may believe that much of truth underlies the sketch which the good Baron Bunsen has drawn of the assembling together of the people at the command of Zoroaster that they might choose between the nature-gods of their fathers and the Lord whom he would have them serve.

Bunsen pictures the assembly as gathered on ' one of the holy hills dedicated to the worship of fire in the neighbourhood of the primeval city of marvels in Central Asia—Bactria, the glorious, now called Balkh.' Thus Zoroaster speaks in the Zend-Avesta:

'Now I shall proclaim to all who have come to listen, the praises of Thee, the all-wise Lord, and the hymns of the good Spirit.

'Hear with your ears what is best, perceive with your mind what is pure, so that every man may for himself choose his tenets before the great doom. May the wise be on our side!

'Those old spirits who are twins, made known what is good and what is evil in thoughts, words and deeds. Those who are good, distinguished between the two, not those who are evil-doers.

'When these two Spirits came together, they made first life and death, so that there should be at last the most wretched life for the bad, but for the good blessedness.

'Of these two Spirits the evil one chose the worst deeds; the kind Spirit, He whose garment is the immovable sky, chose what is right; and they also who faithfully please Ahuramazdâ by good works.

'Let us then be of those who further this world; oh Ahuramazdâ, oh bliss-conferring Asha! (truth). Let our mind be there where wisdom abides.

'Then indeed there will be the fall of the pernicious Druj (falsehood), but in the beautiful abode of Vohumano (the good spirit), of Mazdâ, and Asha, will be gathered for ever those who dwell in good report.

'Oh men, if you cling to these commandments which Mazdâ has given, which are a torment to the wicked and a blessing to the righteous, then there will be victory through them.'

In this old faith there was a belief in two abodes for the departed; heaven, the 'house of the angels' hymns,' and hell, where the wicked were sent. Between the two there was a bridge, over which the souls of the righteous alone passed in safety; the wicked falling into the dark dwelling-place of Ahriman. There are also traces of a resurrection and judgment-day, which will be foretold by Sosiosh, son of Zoroaster, who shall come as the Messiah, or Prophet of Ormuzd, to convert the world and slay the arch-fiend Ahriman, or, as another account relates, to purify the earth by fire, consume all evil, and bring forth from the ashes a new heaven and a new earth, wherein righteousness alone shall dwell.

The few rites and ceremonies which Zoroaster imported into his religion were doubtless such as were familiar to the Aryans when together, and were mainly the offering of *Homa* and of *fire*. The Persian *Homa* or *Haoma* is the same as the Hindu *Soma*, and hymns to it occur in the Zend-Avesta. Ormuzd being the source of light, has for symbols the sun, moon and planets and also fire, which is regarded as his pure creation and therefore most sacred of all things upon earth. The offering of fire has continued to the present day, nor is the flame ever suffered to go out. The Zoroastrians had neither temples nor idols and the fire was kept burning in an enclosed space, the chief rites of worship being performed before it.

The Pârsî still faces some light-giving object, as the sun or fire, when he offers his prayer, and the priests cover their faces when they approach the flame, lest it be defiled by their breath. It is however, untrue to speak of the Pârsîs as worshipping fire; they simply regard it as an emblem of divine power and honour it accordingly. Life being the gift of Ormuzd and therefore dear to him, no sacrifice of blood was offered in the early centuries of the religion, but many corruptions have since crept in and overlaid this once purest and noblest of all the creeds of Asia.

Since death was the dark deed of Ahriman, the dead body has ever been looked upon with horror, and as the Pârsîs believed that the evil demons had secured it, it could not be permitted to pollute the pure elements which Ormuzd had created;

earth, fire and water. So it was put on some exposed place; some 'Tower of Silence' where birds of prey devoured the flesh, and the sunlight bleached the bones, which were afterwards buried in the earth: and such is the practice to this day. But the Zoroastrians had a good hope that the demons had not touched the *pure* soul, which passed away beyond the eastern mountains to the sun-lit paradise of the holy, and there entered into rest.

The history of Persia is full of interest. It was the first among the Aryan nations to rise into importance. Under Cyrus, whose name and deeds are spoken of in the Old Testament, it became a mighty empire, whose boundary stretched from the Indus to Asia Minor, and it was during his reign that the Jews were freed from their captivity at Babylon and returned to Palestine. Darius, Xerxes (the Ahasuerus of Scripture), these are names well-known to us, and under them and other kings Persia remained powerful for centuries until it was conquered by the Arabs, when the old Zoroastrian faith gave place to Mohammadanism.

Professor Max Müller remarks: 'There were periods in the history of the world when the worship of Ormuzd threatened to rise triumphant on the ruins of the temples of all other gods. If the battles of Marathon and Salamis had been lost and Greece had succumbed to Persia, the state religion of the empire of Cyrus, which was the worship of Ormuzd, might have become the religion of the whole civilized world.'

But this was not to be; and there now remain in Asia only a few hundred thousand Pârsîs, some of whom dwell in the old land, while the greater number have settled in and around Bombay.

Their creed is of the simplest kind; it is to fear God, to live a life of pure thoughts, pure words, pure deeds, and to die in the hope of a world to come. It is the creed of those who have lived nearest to God and served Him faithfullest in every age, and wherever they dwell who accept it and practise it, they bear witness to that which makes them children of God and brethren of the prophets, among whom Zoroaster was not the least.

The Jews were carried away as captives to

Babylon some 600 years before Christ, and during the seventy years of their exile there, they came into contact with the Persian religion and derived from it ideas about the immortality of the soul, which their own religion did not contain. They also borrowed from it their belief in a multitude of angels, and in Satan as the ruler over evil spirits. The ease with which man believes in unearthly powers working for his hurt prepares a people to admit into its creed the doctrine of evil spirits, and although it is certain that the Jews had no belief in such spirits before their captivity in Babylon, they spoke of Satan (which means *an adversary*) as a messenger sent from God to watch the deeds of men and accuse them to Him for their wrong-doing. Satan thus becoming by degrees an object of dread, upon whom all the evil which befel men was charged, the minds of the Jews were ripe for accepting the Persian doctrine of Ahriman with his legions of devils. Ahriman became the Jewish Satan, a belief in whom formed part of early Christian doctrine, and is now but slowly dying out. What fearful ills it has caused, history has many a page to tell. The doctrine that Satan, once an angel of light, had been cast from heaven for rebellion against God, and had ever since played havoc among mankind, gave rise to the belief that he and his demons could possess the souls of men and animals at pleasure. Hence grew the belief in wizards and witches, under which millions of creatures, both young and old, were cruelly tortured and put to death.

We turn over the smeared pages of this history in haste, thankful that from such a nightmare the world has wakened, and assured that God tempts us not, neither devil nor wicked angel, but that, as Jesus said, *out of the heart* proceed evil thoughts and all that doth defile. (See on this matter 'Childhood of the World,' pp. 92-94.)

CHAPTER IX.

BUDDHISM.

ALTHOUGH Buddhism, which numbers more followers than any other faith, is hundreds of years younger than the old Hindu religion, we know less about it. We miss in it the gladness which bursts forth in the hymns of the Veda, and to turn from them to it is like reading the sad thoughts in the Book of Ecclesiastes after the cheerful songs of praise in the Book of Psalms. But if clouds and darkness are round about it, and our learned men differ as to what much of it really means, this should not surprise us, since a knowledge of it has come to hand only within the last few years. Even Christians are split up into many sects, because they cannot agree as to the exact meaning of many parts of Scripture, although the loving research of centuries has been given to find it out.

We saw at page 151 how the Brahmans had

coiled their rules round men's souls and bodies, and placed upon them burdens grievous to be borne, without in any way satisfying the cravings of the human spirit. It was against all this that Buddhism revolted, just as in the reign of Henry VIII., the people of England and Germany threw off the shackles of Rome, and made possible the freedom which we now enjoy.

The founder of Buddhism was of princely birth. He was born 628 years before Christ, in Kapilavastu, the royal city of his father, who was ruler of a kingdom north of Oude, in India. He was called *Gautama*, from the tribe to which his family belonged; *Sâkya-Muni*, or 'the monk of the race of Sâkya;' *Siddârtha*, a name given him by his father, and meaning 'He in whom wishes are fulfilled;' and in later years *Buddha*, or more correctly, *the Buddha*; the enlightened; from the root *budh*, to know. (For legends of his birth, see Note I.)

His mother, to whom the future greatness and mighty sway of her boy over men's hearts were made known in a dream, died a few days after his birth. He grew up a beautiful and clever boy, and 'never felt so happy as when he could sit alone lost in thought in the deep shadows of the forest,' although, as he proved when a young man, no unskilled foe to meet in tournament or war. So sad and serious did he become, that his father feared he would grow up a mere dreamer, and, with the view of calling him to an active life, chose a lovely princess to become his wife. He lived happily with her, but was still given to much thought about life and death. Prof. Max Müller tells us that he used to say, 'Nothing on earth is stable, nothing is real. Life is as transitory as a spark of fire, or the sound of a lyre. There must be some supreme intelligence where we could find rest. If I attained it I could bring light to men; if I were free myself, I could deliver the world.' His friends tried to divert his thoughts from these matters by gay scenes and courtly splendours, but it was in vain. At this time he met three sights which deepened his sadness, for they told him what awaited him. These were a feeble old man; a fever-sick and mud-stained man; and a dead body. Afterwards he met a devotee, and resolved, like him, to retire from the world, and thereby, as he vainly thought, escape all that in it is unreal and sad. One night, as he lay upon his couch, a crowd of dancing girls came and displayed their charms before him, but in vain; and when sleep fell upon him, they, weary and vexed, ceased their dancing, and were soon asleep also. Gautama woke at midnight to find them lying around him; and seeing some tossing heavily, some open-mouthed, and others coiled up, it seemed to him as if nought but loathsome bodies filled his splendid apartment, and that all was vanity. That moment he resolved to leave his palace, and while his servant was saddling the fleetest of his horses, he gently opened the room where his wife was sleeping that he might see his child. The mother had one of her hands over its head, and fearing to waken them, he resolved to go, and not look upon his boy till he had become the Buddha. One legend says that he had scarcely crossed the threshold when the tempter met him and sought to thwart his purpose by promising him rule over all the kingdoms of this world; but Gautama would not yield, yet from that day the tempter ceased not to attack the holy man. He went among the Brahmans to see if their teaching would lighten his burden; he did what they told him, performed their rites and ceremonies, but these brought him no peace. He left them and retired to a small village, where, after practising the most severe rites, the repute of his sanctity brought to him five disciples, with whom he remained six years. Seeing that such a life led not to perfection, but was useless and selfish, giving nothing and taking all, he returned to more cheerful ways, and, still pursuing his thinking, had his reward. As he sat one day beneath a tree, a great joy came to him, for knowledge burst in upon him by which he became Buddha, the man who knew.

While fasting under the tree during the sacred period of seven times seven days and nights the demon of wickedness attacked him a second time, even using force, but was defeated by the power of the ten great virtues of Buddha, the weapons of the evil one and of his soldiers being changed into beautiful flowers as they fell upon Buddha, and the rocks becoming nosegays as they were hurled at him; whereupon the spirits who had watched over his birth and who now followed his life on earth rent the air with shouts of joy at his victory. Afterwards the tempter sent his three daughters, one a winning girl; one a blooming virgin; and one a middle-aged beauty, to allure him, but they could not. Buddha was proof against all the demon's arts, and his only trouble was whether it were well or not to preach his doctrines to men. Feeling how hard to gain was that which he had gained, and how enslaved men were by their passions so that they might neither listen to him nor understand him, he had well nigh resolved to be silent, but at the last deep compassion for all beings made him resolve to tell his secret to mankind that they too might be free, and he thus became the founder of the most popular religion of ancient or modern times. The spot where Buddha obtained his knowledge became one of the most sacred places in India. He first preached at Benares, or, as they say, 'turned the wheel of the law,' a phrase which may have given rise to the wheels on which some of his words are inscribed and which are set in motion by wind or water. He met with great opposition from the

Brahmans, but kept on his way, converting the high and the low until in his eighty-fifth year he died peacefully while sitting under a tree. His remains were burnt amidst great pomp and quarrels arose for the possession of the fragments. They were at last divided into eight portions, over each of which a *tope* (a Hindu word for a bell-shaped building raised over relics) was built. Of course the usual legends teeming with stories of wonderful miracles grew around his memory, and this notwithstanding that he told his disciples the only true wonder was to 'hide their good deeds and confess before men their sins.' The myths and traditions of the Buddhists about the universe and the things therein are absurd in the extreme.

Very soon after his death a general council of his disciples was held to fix the doctrines and rules of the religion. Buddha had written nothing himself, and the council is said to have chosen from his followers those who remembered most of his teaching. It is interesting to note that among these were two men, one of deep earnestness and zeal; the other of most sweet nature, loving Buddha much and most beloved by him; reminding us of two of Christ's disciples, Peter and John.

Two other councils were afterwards held for the correction of errors that had crept into the faith, and for sending missionaries into other lands. The last of these councils is said to have been held 251 years before Christ, so that long before Christianity was founded we have this great religion with its sacred traditions of Buddha's words, its councils and its missions, besides, as we shall presently see, many things strangely like the rites of the Roman Catholic Church.

The Buddhist scriptures are called the 'Tripitaka,'* or 'three baskets,' being in three parts. The first 'pitaka' contains rules of discipline; the second, the discourses of Buddha; and the third treats of philosophy and the subtle doctrines of the religion. The words of Buddha, handed on from age to age and preserved in the memories of men, were at last set down in writing. They grew, as our Scriptures have grown, much entering into them which Buddha never said, but all the writings at

* See Note K.

last received as the sacred records of his teaching and religion.

Among the traditions concerning Buddha, there is one which tells of a young mother whose child died and whose dead body, in her great love and sorrow, she clasped to her bosom, and went about from house to house asking if any one would give her some medicine for it. The neighbours thought her mad, but a wise man, seeing that she could not or would not understand the law of death, said to her, 'My good girl, I cannot myself give medicine for it, but I know of a doctor who can attend to it.' She asked who it was, and was sent by the wise man to Buddha. After doing homage to him, she said, 'Lord and master, do you know any medicine that will be good for my boy?' Buddha replied that he did, and told her to fetch a handful of mustard seed which must be taken from a house where no son, husband, parent, or slave had died. Then the woman went in search, but no such house could she find, for whenever she asked if there had died any of those, the answer came from one, 'I have lost a son;' from another, 'I have lost my parents;' and from all,

'Lady, the living are few, but the dead are many.' At last, not finding any house where death had not been, the truth broke in upon her, and leaving the dead body of her boy in a forest, she returned to Buddha, and told her tale. He said to her, 'You thought that you alone had lost a son; the law of death is that among all living creatures there is nothing that abides,' and when he had finished preaching the law, the woman became his disciple.

Once upon a time Buddha lived in a village, and in the sowing season, went with his bowl in hand to the place where food was being given by a Brahman, who seeing him, spoke thus:

'O priest, I both plough and sow, and having ploughed and sown, I eat; you also, O priest, should plough and sow, and having ploughed and sown, you should eat.'

'I too, O Brahman, plough and sow, and having ploughed and sown, I eat,' said Buddha.

'But we see neither the yoke, nor plough, nor ploughshare, nor goad, nor oxen, of the venerable Gautama. . . .

'Being questioned by us as to your ploughing, speak in such a manner as we may know of your ploughing.'

The Buddha replied: 'For my cultivation, faith is the seed; penance the rain; wisdom my yoke and plough; modesty the shaft for the plough; mind the string; presence-of mind my ploughshare and goad.'

Then the Brahman offered him rice boiled in milk from a golden vessel.

In a chapter very popular among the Buddhists of Ceylon, the demon Álavaka is said to have asked Buddha, 'What is the best wealth to a man in this world? What thing well done produces happiness? Of savoury things, which is indeed the most savoury? The life of one who lives in what manner, do they say, is the best?'

Buddha answered: 'Faith is the best wealth to a man here. The observing well the law produces happiness. Truth is indeed the most savoury of all savoury things. The living endowed with wisdom, they say, is the best of all modes of living.'

On another occasion, when asked what was the greatest blessing, Buddha said:

'The succouring of mother and father, the cherishing of child and wife, and the following of a lawful calling, this is the greatest blessing.

'The giving alms, a religious life, aid rendered to relations, blameless acts, this is the greatest blessing.

'The abstaining from sins and the avoiding them, the eschewing of intoxicating drink, diligence in good deeds, reverence and humility, contentment and gratefulness, this is the greatest blessing.

. . . 'Those who having done these things, become invincible on all sides, attain happiness on all sides. This is the greatest blessing.'

There is a discourse of Buddha's which some have called, from the place where it was preached, his 'sermon on the mount,' but it lacks clearness, nor could it be set down in language easy to grasp. The extracts from Buddhist sacred books just given show how forcefully Buddha could put much meaning into few words, and of this there is rich proof in a book called the 'Dhammapada,' or 'Path of Virtue,' which is believed to contain his sayings. For example:

'He who lives looking for pleasures only, his senses uncontrolled, idle and weak, Mâra (the tempter) will certainly overcome him, as the wind throws down a weak tree.'

'Let the wise man guard his thoughts, they are difficult to perceive, very artful, and they rush wherever they list; thoughts well guarded bring happiness.'

'As the bee collects nectar, and departs without injuring the flower, or its colour and scent, so let the sage dwell on earth.'

'Like a beautiful flower, full of colour but without scent, are the fine but fruitless words of him who does not act accordingly. But like a beautiful flower, full of colour and full of scent, are the fine and fruitful words of him who acts accordingly.'

'He who lives a hundred years, vicious and unrestrained, a life of one day is better if a man is virtuous and reflecting.

'Let no man think lightly of evil, saying in his heart, It will not come near unto me. Even by the falling of water-drops a water-pot is filled; the fool becomes full of evil even if he gathers it little by little.'

'Not to commit any sin, to do good, and to purify one's mind, that is the teaching of the Awakened.' (This is one of the most solemn verses among the Buddhists).

'Let us live happily then, not hating those who hate us! Let us dwell free from hatred among men who hate!
'Let us live happily then, free from greed among the greedy! Let us dwell free from greed among men who are greedy!
'Let us live happily then, though we call nothing our own! We shall be like the bright gods, feeding on happiness!'

Buddhism became the state religion of India in the reign of King Asoka, (who ascended the throne about 268 years before Christ), and continued so for nearly nine centuries, until, from causes by no means clear, it was driven therefrom, and has since found its followers mainly among those great races of Asia which are neither Aryan nor Semitic, but which may be roughly classed as Mongol. It is one of the three State religions of China; it is the religion of Tibet, and spreads northwards to the confines of Swedish Lapland and southwards into Burmah, embracing nearly the whole of Eastern Asia, including Japan, in which island it is, however, not the state religion. The island of Ceylon supplies us with much of our knowledge about Buddha, and is rich in Buddhist architecture, cave-temples, shrines, ruined cities and relics, chiefest among which are a so-called tooth of Buddha, and a famous tree, nearly 2200 years old, which is a branch of the tree under which he sat when he became the Enlightened. Buddhism as a great *religion* is a very different thing from Buddhism as a *philosophy*, and its marvellous success was surely not owing to Buddha's dreamy speculations about the misery of life, and to his dreary teaching as to the best way of escape therefrom.

We saw that he strove to find in this world of unrest something that was lasting, the knowledge of which might release him from change and decay. Now the great doctrines of the deeper part of his religion are given in what he called 'the four sublime truths.'

They assert that there is pain; that pain comes

through the desire or passion for things that cannot be ours for long; that both the pain and the desire can be ended by Nirvâna, to which in the fourth truth Buddha shows the right way. Many learned men think that by this Buddha meant *nothingness,* ceasing to be, the soul being 'blown out' like the flame of a candle.

The four paths to this way are as follows:

He has entered the *first* path who sees the evils arising from separate existence, and who believes in Buddha and in the power of his system alone to obtain salvation, that is, deliverance from separate existence.

He has entered the *second* path who, besides the above, is free from lust and evil to others.

He has entered the *third* path who is further free from all kinds of evil desires, from ignorance, doubt, wrong belief and hatred; while

He has arrived at the *fourth* path who is entirely free from sin ('has cast it away as if it were a burden'), and passions, by which are meant the lust of the flesh, the love of existence, and the defilements of wrong-belief and ignorance.

The four paths have also been summed up in

eight steps or divisions: right views, right thoughts, right speech, right actions, right living, right exertion, right recollection, right meditation.

After these doctrines there follow ten commandments, of which the first five apply to all people, and the rest chiefly to such as set themselves apart for a religious life. They are, not to kill; not to steal; not to commit adultery; not to lie; not to get drunk; to abstain from late meals; from public amusements; from expensive dress; from large beds; and to accept neither gold nor silver.

It is easy to see that the more difficult part of Buddha's teaching, which was largely caused by the love common to Hindus for knotty questions, and by his study of the systems of the Brahmans, might give rise to endless speculations among the learned few, but would never move or draw to itself the unlearned masses of men.

The success of Buddhism was in this: It was a protest against the powers of the priests; it to a large degree broke down caste by declaring that all men were equal, and by allowing any one desiring to live a holy life to become a priest.

'Not from birth,' said Buddha, ' does one become a Vasala (slave), not from birth does one become a Brahman. By bad conduct does one become a Vasala, by good conduct does one become a Brahman.' It abolished sacrifices; made it the duty of all men to honour their parents and care for their children, to be kind to the sick and poor and sorrowing, to forgive their enemies and return good for evil; it spread a spirit of charity abroad which encompassed the lowest life as well as the highest, bidding men

> 'Never to blend their pleasure or their pride
> With sorrow of the meanest thing that lives.'

This was why the common people heard it gladly. They could not soar into the upper clouds, but needed some faith and hope by which to do the hard work of life; and when life was over, they looked for a paradise where they would be delivered from care and suffering. Towards such the millions of Buddhists look this day, for

> 'Whatever crazy sorrow saith,
> No life that breathes with human breath
> Has ever truly longed for death.

'Tis life, whereof our nerves are scant,
Oh life, not death, for which we pant;
More life, and fuller, that we want.'

The teaching of Buddha, like that of Christ, has been changed and overlaid with doctrines foreign to it by the nations who have accepted it, and the forms of worship adopted by Buddhists vary in the different countries, but consist mainly in adoration of the statues of Buddha and of his relics, he being, in their view, that which any man may become by practice of the four sublime truths and the commandments. In Buddhism as a *philosophy* the being of God is not denied; it is ignored, nothing is said about it: as a *religion*, its millions of followers believe in many gods. We have seen how closely the teaching of Buddha's law of mercy and charity is like to that of Christ's, being in short the fruit of the loving nature of each of these holy men; and another feature, hinted at above, is the likeness between certain rites of Buddhism and Christianity. When the Roman Catholic missionaries first met the Buddhist monks they were shocked when they saw that their heads were shaven, that they knelt before images, that they worshipped relics, wore strings of beads, used bells and holy water, and had confession of sin. They believed that the devil, as the father of all mischief and deceit, had tempted these men to dress themselves in the clothes of Catholics and mock their solemn practices; whereas it seems likely that there had been some connection in the past, the younger religion borrowing from the older.

Of the strange mode by which the Tibetans, on the death of the Grand Lama, who is their high priest, and regarded as infallible, like the Pope, elect his successor, into whom they believe his soul passes, space forbids an account. Monasteries for men and nunneries for women still exist, and especially in Tibet, vast numbers of monks are found; while the huge and now deserted monasteries and temples cut in the solid rock, and of which hundreds exist in India, show how mightily a system, which had been thought to belong to Christianity only, had formed part of Buddhism two thousand years ago.

CHAPTER X.

THE RELIGIONS OF CHINA.

ALTHOUGH we are still in the East, we leave its gorgeous dazzlements behind, and once within the walls of China come amongst scenes where song gives place to prose and golden romance to sober fact; where the people's faces, their houses, their junks and their hand-writing, seem made after one pattern.

On the soil of this great country there is crowded nearly half the human race. The manners and customs of the Chinese are those of their ancestors hundreds of years ago. Empires have risen and fallen around them, but they remain the same, nor have the races that have broken through their Great Wall and forced rulers upon them altered their laws or their language. The mariner's compass; printing; gunpowder and other arts, were known to them long before they were in use in Europe. Theirs is a land where everything seems topsy-turvy. The soldiers wear petticoats, use fans and fight the enemy at night with lanterns; the people have fireworks by daylight; white is the colour used in mourning; boats are drawn by men and carriages are moved by sails; while visiting cards are four feet long and painted red! In the high honour paid to learning the Chinese teach us a lesson. The lowest among them can rise to the highest offices in the state, these being given, not to the best-born, but to those who have passed with the greatest merit the public examinations; so that knowledge is the road to power.

The ancient inhabitants of China, like the races with whom they are thought to be allied, were worshippers of the powers of nature and of the spirits of their ancestors, and these still largely enter into the religions of China. There is a State worship kept up by the Emperor and his court, in which sacrifices are offered to the heaven and earth, to the spirits of sages, rulers and learned men; also of mountains, fields and rivers; while each household has its family spirits to whom honour and reverence are paid. And behind all this there looms a supreme power, lord of the sky, 'ancestor of all things,' who is however as vague a being to the Chinese as is Brahm to the Hindus.

China has three national religions; Buddhism, which was admitted as a religion of the State 65 years after Christ, the Chinese name of Buddha being Fo; Taoism; and Confucianism.

The three religions are often professed by the same person, and there is none of that bitter feeling between the believers in different creeds which exists so much among Christians, Muslims and others. This is, however, owing to the lack of earnestness; for they who feel deeply concerning what they believe cannot be careless regarding what they think are the errors of others.

Lao-tse, the founder of Taoism, lived between 500 and 600 years before Christ, and was an altogether different man from Confucius. He was a thinker, not a worker, seeking to unravel those same problems which perplexed Buddha, and what there is in the Chinese belief of a spiritual kind may have been aided by the teaching of Lao-tse. Confucius is said to have visited him and confessed that he could not understand him. Taoism has become mixed up with magic and other senseless beliefs, and its priests are for the most part ignorant men, so that it has no great hold upon the Chinese.

Their great teacher and lawgiver, whose 'writings and life have given the law to Chinese thought,' is K'ung-Foo-Tse, 'the master K'ung,' whose name has been Latinized into Confucius. He is their patron saint; his descendants are held in special honour; the most famous temple in the empire is built over his grave, while hundreds of other temples to his memory abound, and thousands of animals are sacrificed on the two yearly festivals sacred to that memory. Each one of the thousands who compete in the great examinations must know the whole system of Confucius and commit his doctrines to heart.

This man, who was reviled in life, but whose influence sways the hundreds of millions of China, was born 551 years before Christ, not far from the time when Cyrus became king of Persia and the Jews returned from Babylon, and a few years before the death of Buddha. He lost his father, who was an old man and an officer of state in the kingdom of Loo, now a Chinese province, when he was three years old; but his mother trained him with tender care, and he is said to have shown from an early age great love for learning and for the laws and lore of his country. At the time when Confucius lived, China was divided into a number of petty kingdoms whose rulers were ever quarrelling, and although he became engaged in various public situations of trust, the disorder of the state at last caused him to resign them, and he retired to another part of the country. He then continued the life of a public teacher, instructing men in the simple moral truths by which he sought to govern his own life. The purity of that life, and the example of veneration for the old laws which he set, gathered round him many grave and thoughtful men, who worked with him for the common good. He afterwards returned to Loo, and remaining for some years without office, became in his 50th year a minister of state, and great success attended his wise rule; but at last the wild excesses of the court upturned his good laws, and he had to resign his place. Poverty and other ills came upon him, few heeded his words of wisdom, and after many wanderings, he returned to his native land a despised and poor man. He spent the remainder of his life in editing the sacred books of China, and in writing some additions to them, and passed away in the seventy-third year of his age.

His system can scarcely be called a religion, and yet that is the best name for it, because it teaches men how to live. Four things he is said to have taught: learning, morals, devotion of soul and reverence. He counselled all to be sincere, just, loving, careful of duty to themselves and others, and observant of ancient laws and rites. He had nothing to say about God or another life. Here and there he speaks in vague words of 'heaven,' a power whose emblem is the sky, but not of One to whom praises should ascend, and towards Whom the love of children should be felt. This was not because Confucius was an unbeliever, for he, of all men, had reverence for the sacred, unknown power that underlies all things, but because his nature was so beautifully simple and sincere that he would not pretend to knowledge of that which he felt was beyond human reach and thought. This was shown in his reply to a disciple who asked him concerning death. 'While you do not know life, how can you know about death?'

His life was given to teaching a few great truths, obedience to which he believed would bring happiness to man. He says of himself: 'At fifteen years, I had my mind bent on learning. At thirty, I stood firm. At forty, I had no doubts. At fifty, I knew the decrees of heaven. At sixty, everything I heard I easily understood. At seventy, the desires of my heart no longer transgressed the law.'

The sacred books of China are called the *Kings*,* and are five in number, containing treatises on morals, books of rites, poems and history. They are of great age, perhaps as old as the earliest hymns of the Rig-Veda, and are free from any impure thoughts. *King* means the warp threads of a web. The name is given as showing

* See Note L.

that which is woven together; like the use of our word *text*, which comes from the Latin *textum*, 'that which is woven.'

These books, which were deeply studied by Confucius, teach that there is one Supreme Being, everywhere present, all-seeing, who commands right deeds, pure thoughts and watchfulness over the tongue. 'For a blemish may be taken out of a diamond by carefully polishing it; but if your words have the least blemish, there is no way to efface that.' 'Heaven penetrates to the bottom of our hearts, like light into a dark chamber. We must conform ourselves to it until we are like two instruments of music tuned to the same pitch. Our passions shut up the door of our souls against God.'

Such are among the wise words of these most ancient books, restored by Confucius to their rightful place. I should like ample space to quote many of his own pithy sayings, which are given in the first of the four *Shoo*, meaning *writings* or *books*, compiled by his disciples, but a few must suffice.

'The Master said, "Shall I teach you what knowledge is? When you know a thing, to hold that you know it, and when you do not know a thing, to allow that you do not know it; this is knowledge."'

'To see what is right and not to do it is want of courage.'

'Worship as though the Deity were present.'

'He who offends against Heaven has none to whom he can pray.'

'If my mind is not engaged in my worship, it is as though I worshipped not.'

'Coarse rice for food, water to drink, the bended arm for a pillow,—happiness may be enjoyed even with these; but without virtue, both riches and honour seem to me like the passing cloud.'

'Grieve not that men know not you; grieve that you know not men.'

'A good man is serene; a bad man always in fear.'

'There may be fair words and an humble countenance when there is little virtue.'

'One of his disciples said,' "If you, Master, do not speak, what shall we, your disciples, have to read?" The Master said, "Does Heaven speak? The four seasons pursue their courses, and all things are continually being produced; but does Heaven say anything?"'

'In the Book of Poetry are three hundred pieces, but the design of them all may be embraced in that one sentence, "Have no depraved thoughts."' (This reminds us of the saying of the later Jewish Rabbis that all the 613 precepts of the Law were summed up in the words, 'The just shall live by his faith.')

'If a man in the morning hear the right way, he may die in the evening without regret.'

'Tsze-kung said, "What I do not wish men to do to me,

I also wish not to do to men." The Master said, "You have not attained to that."'

Such is the power of words, that those uttered by this intensely earnest man, whose work was ended only by death, have kept alive throughout the vast empire of China a reverence for the past and a sense of duty to the present which have made the Chinese the most orderly and moral people in the world. But to 'the mighty hopes that make us men,' they are strangers. Theirs is a dull, plodding life, and one can hardly say of them what Pope wrote of the Indian:

> 'To be, contents his natural desire,
> He asks no angel's wing, no seraph's fire,'

for their hold on life is slender, and it is a great matter with them to have their coffins ready. They, however, speak of the dead as 'ascended to the sky,' and have a great horror of being beheaded, in the belief that there can be no hereafter for a headless trunk.

It is only of late years, and that not by the best means, that parts of their vast empire have been entered by foreigners; but we must hope that when the religion of Christ becomes known among them they will feel that it lends just that motive and aim to the life of man which their religions lack, and which is needed to make life complete.

CHAPTER XI

THE SEMITIC NATIONS.

ALL that has been said about the common descent of the Aryan or Indo-European nations applies to the Semitic nations. Their languages are shown to be even more closely related than the Aryan languages and afford clear proof of a time when the ancestors of the Semitic peoples lived together, speaking the same tongue and worshipping the same gods. When further research is made we may look for as vivid a picture of old Semitic life as that which we have of old Aryan manners and customs.

Under the name *Semitic* or *Shemitic*, meaning people descended from Shem, one of the sons of Noah (a term which by no means truly describes them), there are included the Jews and other Syrian tribes, the Arabs, Assyrians, Babylonians, Phœnicians and Carthaginians. Of the home from which the old Semitic races migrated we cannot speak with certainty; it may have been in the country watered by the rivers Euphrates and Tigris, or in some part of Arabia.

These nations have filled an important place in human history, but they have never spread themselves over the earth as have the Aryans. They have been great in religion, in science and in commerce, the cities which they founded, Jerusalem, Nineveh, Babylon, Tyre, and their settlements in Carthage and Spain, reminding us what a splendid and deathless story their records tell.

In the ancient worship of the Semitic races before they separated, there are clear traces that the names of their chief gods had been fixed.

These names mostly express moral qualities; that is, instead of a god of fire, or storm, or sky, we have the Strong, the Exalted, the Lord, the King, etc. One of the highest and oldest names was *El*, meaning strong. 'It occurs in the Babylonian inscriptions as *Ilu*, God, and in the very name of *Bab-il*, the gate or temple of *Il*. We have it in *Beth-el*, the house of God, and in many other names. The same *El* was worshipped at Byblus by the Phœnicians and was called there 'the son of heaven and earth.' *Eloah* is the same word as the

Arabic *Ilâh*, God : *Ilâh*, without the article, means a god in general ; with the article *Al-Ilâh* or *Allâh*, it becomes the name of the God of Mohammad, as it was the name of the God of Abraham and of Moses.' Another famous name is *Baal* or *Bel*, *the lord*. He was not only a supreme god among the Assyrians, Babylonians and Phœnicians, but was a frequent object of worship by the Jews.

Then we have the Hebrew *Melech*, king, which is the *Moloch* of the Phœnicians, to whom children were sacrificed by their own parents, a horrible practice which they carried with them to Carthage and other places.

These and other names were common to the undivided Semitic people, but it is thought that the name *Jah*, *Jahveh* or *Jehovah*, was used by the Jews only. Be this as it may, 'Hebrew, Syriac and Arabic point to a common source as much as Sanskrit, Greek and Latin.'

But the ancient history of the mighty empires of the East does not form part of my subject, and manuals of Jewish history especially are so numerous that it is needless to give what must be, at the best, only a meagre account.

We must ever feel the deepest interest in the Jews, because while Aryan blood flows in our veins, our Christian religion has come from a Semitic race. The long line of noble men to whom the Jewish nation has given birth from the time of its founder Abraham to the age when Jesus Christ and his apostles lived; the fearless witness which since the days of its captivity it has borne to the lofty truth that 'there is One God and none other but He,' must ever give to its scattered people a large place in our veneration and our love. Only it must be no blind, but a pure and true veneration, born of careful study of all that they have been and of all that they have done. We must treat their history as we treat every other history, and not think that they could be dearer to God than those who, like the Persian Aryans, forsook Him less to worship many gods.

Of the Semitic religions those that concern us in the present day are only the Jewish and the Mohammadan, of which latter some account will now follow.

CHAPTER XII.

MOHAMMADANISM, OR ISLÁM.

THIS religion, which is the guide in life and the support in death of one hundred and fifty millions of our fellow creatures; which, like Christianity, has its missionaries scattered over the globe, and offers itself as a faith needed by all men; which for hundreds of years has had firm hold upon the sacred places of Palestine so dear to Jew and Christian, is worth careful study. *Islám*, which is its correct name, comes from a word meaning in the first instance 'to be at rest, to have done one's duty, to be at perfect peace,' and is commonly held to mean 'submission to the will and commandments of God.'

Muslim, the name given to its believers (spelt also Moslem, Muslem, &c.), comes from *Islám*, and means ' a righteous man.'

While we know very little about the lives of the founders of some religions already sketched, and that little so mixed up with fable and legend as to make it hard work to sift the false from the true, nearly all the facts of Mohammad's life are well known to us, and are supported by the witness of thousands who knew him for many years.

And the value of Islám, the youngest of the great religions, is, that we are able to see how its first simple form became overlaid with legend and foolish superstition, and thus learn how, in like manner, myth and fable have grown around more ancient religions.

For example: although Mohammad came into the world like other children, wonderful things were said to have taken place at his birth; one legend being that angels took him from the arms of his nurse, drew his heart from his bosom, and then squeezed from it the black drop of sin which is in every child of Adam.

He never claimed to be a perfect man; he did not pretend to foretell events or to work miracles. He said, 'My miracle is the Korân, which shall remain for ever,' and he pointed to those great signs in heaven and earth, greater than the wonders said to have been wrought by men,—the sun, and moon, and stars; the day and the night; the mountains which keep the earth steady (an old Arab notion); the water that slakes man's thirst and the cattle which change the grass into milk, as parts of one great, never-ceasing miracle.

In spite of all this, his followers said of him, while he was yet living, that he worked wonders, and they believed the golden vision, hinted at in the Korân (concerning which Mohammadan tradition tells how, clothed in robe and turban of light, he rode by night upon the lightning to Jerusalem, and then ascending to heaven, passed through the dwellings of the prophets into the presence of the Unseen, where stillness was, and nothing heard, 'except the silent sound of the reed wherewith the decrees of God are written on the tablets of fate'), to have been a real event, although Mohammad said over and over again that it was but a dream. When he died, the people would not believe it; the places where he had trod became to them the holiest spots on earth, and the words which he had spoken, the very words of God. Thus it has been with other prophets of the Most High. They have been too great for smaller men to understand, have towered too high for them to measure, and when they have passed away, have been looked upon as gods that 'have come down in the likeness of men.'

Mohammad has suffered much both from friend and foe. The former, who asked him to do something to prove his high mission, as the Jews asked Jesus for a sign, willingly believed anything they were told of him; the latter thought that nothing too vile or bad could be said of him. A story was invented that he had trained a dove to pick peas from his ear, so that it might be taken for an angel bringing him messages from God! Martin Luther called him 'a horrid devil,' and to this day most Christians believe that he was a shameless impostor. Mohammad was a man, and therefore not free from sin. Although that sin stained the later years of his life, he was no cheat or false prophet, but from the day when his strong soul burst the bonds of forty years' silence, a preacher of the eternal truth; 'La Ellâh Ellâla,' 'There is no god but God.'

'By their fruits ye shall know them.' A

religion which has fed the heart-hunger of millions of men for nigh 1300 years cannot have been cradled in fraud. It did not grow without a struggle, for if stones and sneers could have killed it, it would have died during Mohammad's life-time.

Mohammad was born at Mekkeh, or, as it is usually spelt, Mecca, in Arabia, 571 years after Christ. His father, who died before his birth, was poor, but of a noble tribe, the Koreish, who were guardians of the famous sacred stone of the Kaabah. As he lost his mother when he was six years old, he was left to the care of relatives. He was a sickly boy, subject to fits, which troubled him in after years; but he had to begin work, tending flocks, at an early age. He was of a nature given to silence and fondness for being alone, caring to have for company only his own thoughts and nature. The grim, lonely desert, and the stars, that shine their brightest in the East, fed his sense of wonder and opened the ear of his soul to any voice that spake the meaning of all that he saw. He could neither read nor write, and so the more used eye and ear, gathering much knowledge of men and things from journeys with his uncle into Syria. Although sweet-natured, faithful and truthful, he was, perhaps owing to the fits which distressed him, often cast down and gloomy; but in his bright moods he would enter with zest into the glad, free life of children, play with them, and tell them the gorgeous tales of which the East has so rich a store. He lived a most simple life; his dress and food were of the plainest; he mended his own clothes; waited upon himself; and was ever ready to share his meal with the poor. When he was twenty-four years old, he entered the service of a rich widow, who afterwards became his wife and bore him children.

Now we come to the great event of his life. As he neared middle age, his gloom deepened, and he more and more fled from men. It had been his custom for years to spend in prayer and meditation the sacred month during which the Arab tribes laid down their weapons, and in his fortieth year he retired to a small cave on Mount Hira, a huge barren rock standing by itself in the desert, some three miles from Mecca.

Dreams and visions, strange sights and sounds,

as he verily believed, came to him there, and one night a voice called to him, 'Cry, in the name of thy Lord,' and bade him spread the true religion among men by writing.

'Such light had come, as it could, to illumine the darkness of this wild Arab soul. A confused, dazzling splendour, as of life and heaven, in the great darkness which threatened to be death: he called it revelation and (said it was the voice of) the angel Gabriel,—who of us yet can know what to call it? It is the "inspiration of the Almighty" that giveth us understanding.' He went home tremblingly and told his wife, who at once hailed him as the prophet of the nation.

The Arabs are to-day what they were hundreds of years ago; lovers of freedom, temperate, good-hearted; but withal crafty, revengeful, dishonest. They are very fond of music and poetry, and the rise of a poet in any tribe is a matter for great rejoicing. Not much is known about their religion in the days of 'Ignorance,' as they call the time before Islám, for until Mohammad came their history is almost a blank. They believed in many gods and worshipped sun, moon, trees and stones, the most famous among the last being the Black stone of the Kaaba, round which 365 idols were placed. This stone, which travellers tell us is an aerolite (or *air-stone*, as the word means, which has fallen from space upon the earth), is said to have been one of the precious stones of Paradise and to have dropped to the earth with Adam; once white, it has become black through the kisses of sinful men or through the silent tears which it has shed for their sins. Arab legend also tells that the building which encloses it was erected by Abraham and Ishmael. To the place where it stands the Muslims all over the world turn five times every day in prayer to God.

Some of the Arab tribes had strange notions about a future state. They would tie a camel to a man's tomb and leave it without food. If it got away the man was lost for ever; but if not, he would find it there at the day of judgment and could mount on it to Paradise.

There had been settlements of Jews among the Arabs from a very early period, and their religion had been embraced by a few. At the time when

Mohammad appeared, there were also dotted here and there societies of Jews and Christian sects who had sought refuge in the pathless desert from the cruel power of Rome. But the Christians who had come thither wasted their strength in vain and foolish wrangling. The soul of Christianity, the pure, sweet spirit which they might have kept by learning of Christ, had fled from their midst, and they were quarreling with each other about the structure of the dead and worthless body in which that soul had dwelt. Still earlier than any of these there had come sun-worshippers from Chaldea and Zoroastrians from Persia.

From this we may gather what strangely varied beliefs found a home in Arabia, and also see how the many Jewish and Christian ideas became mingled with Islám.

There had risen before Mohammad men who preached against the old pagan creeds, but they were only forerunners of this mightier prophet who was nursing his soul in secret, who

'Yet should bring some worthy thing for waiting souls to see,
Some sacred word that he had heard their light and life to be.'

Mohammad did not claim to preach a new faith, but the 'religion of Abraham,' whom he said 'was neither a Jew nor a Christian, but pious and righteous and no idolater,' and whom he places among the six chief prophets chosen by God to make known His truth. Mohammad said that these were Adam, Noah, Abraham, Moses, Jesus and himself. He made known an Almighty and Allwise God, Who had spoken through these prophets, and to the lasting honour of Mohammad he spake no slighting word of those who came before him. Although his knowledge of Christ was obtained from some childish and false gospels which have long since been treated by Christians as worthless, and although he knew nothing of Christ's holy life and beautiful teaching as given in the Four Gospels, he paid him great honour and believed that he worked miracles.

Muslims have not treated Christ as we have treated Mohammad, for the devout among them never utter his name without adding the touching words, 'on whom be peace,' and in the great mosque at El Medíneh or Medina there is a grave kept for him by the side of the prophet, it being a Muslim belief that Christ will one day return to earth to establish everywhere the religion of Mohammad, who will appear shortly before the day of judgment. Mohammad borrowed from the religion of the Jews, of which he had only a hearsay knowledge, the belief in good and bad angels, some of the laws relating to marriage, fasting, &c., and there were certain customs so closely intertwined with the pagan faith of his countrymen that he wisely sought not to remove some of them, but to purify them. He abolished the frightful practice of killing female children and made the family tie more respected, although to this day its looseness is a great blot upon Islám. He permitted the worship of the Kaaba stone, and the pilgrimages thereto, to be continued. In like manner the Roman Catholic missionaries, when they came to Northern Europe, made use of the best of what they found in the old Teutonic religion and worked it into their own. Where sacred trees had stood, they raised crosses; where holy wells had been dug and the babbling spring was a deity, they built churches and abbeys; where love and piety had named flower and insect after the 'lady' Freyja, goddess of plenty, they put the Virgin Mary in her stead. The goddess Hel, who in a realm of bitter cold received the souls of those who died of old age or disease (for only to those who died in battle was there given endless mirth and feasting in Valhalla with the Alfadir, Odin) was changed from a person to a place where heat, not cold, is the torment. In the bleak North, life without fire is dreary, which explains why Hel was pictured as ruling in a *cold* region.

But we must return to Mohammad, not forgetting to say that Mecca had been a place of very great note long before his time, the Arabs having a tradition that it was the birthplace of their tribes. Near to the Kaaba, there is the well Zemzem, said to be fed by the spring that opened before Hagar's eyes when Ishmael was a-nigh dead with thirst, and when, in a mother's mad despair, she cast him from her that she might not see him die. The legend further relates that they settled on the spot with a tribe who were passing by, and thus arose the sacred city of Mecca.

Mohammad counselled men to live a good life,

and to strive after the mercy of God by fasting, charity, and prayer, which he called 'the key of paradise.'

This is one among many passages in the Korân counselling men to prayer:

'Observe prayer at sunset, till the first darkening of the night, and the daybreak reading—for the daybreak reading hath its witnesses.

'And watch unto it in the night . . . and say, "O my Lord, cause me to enter (Mecca) with a perfect entry, and to come forth with a perfect forthcoming, and give me from thy presence a helping power."'

There is preserved a sermon on charity, said to have been preached by Mohammad, which is so beautiful that it deserves a place beside the apostle Paul's sweet words in 1 Corinthians xiii., while in reading it, we think of that touching saying by Jesus as to the Eye that sees with approval a gift to the thirsty, although that gift be but 'a cup of cold water.'

"When God made the earth, it shook to and fro till He put mountains on it to keep it firm. Then the angels asked, "O God, is there anything in Thy creation stronger than these mountains?" And God replied, "Iron is stronger than the mountains, for it breaks them." "And is there anything in Thy creation stronger than iron?" "Yes, fire is stronger than iron, for it melts it." "Is there anything stronger than fire?" "Yes, water, for it quenches fire." "Is there anything stronger than water?" "Yes, wind, for it puts water in motion." "O our Sustainer, is there anything in thy creation stronger than wind?" "Yes, a good man giving alms; if he give it with his right hand and conceal it from his left, he overcomes all things. Every good act is charity; your smiling in your brother's face; your putting a wanderer in the right road; your giving water to the thirsty is charity; exhortation to another to do right is charity. A man's true wealth hereafter is the good he has done in this world to his fellow-men. When he dies, people will ask, What property has he left behind him? But the angels will ask, What good deeds has he sent before him?"'

Mohammad commanded his followers to make no image of any living thing, to show mercy to the weak and orphaned, and kindness to brutes; to abstain from gambling, smoking tobacco and the use of strong drink.

The great truth which he strove to make real to them was that God is one, that, as the Korân says, 'they surely are infidels who say that God is the third of three, for there is no God but one God.'

To return to the story of his life. It says very much for the pure motives that swayed him that his own nearest friends were the first to believe in him. Others called him fool, mad poet, stargazer, but he held on his way, although for some time with scant success, his followers being, up to the fourth year of his mission, few and humble. It is said that he was one day talking with a rich man whom he wished to convert, when a poor blind man came up and asked to be taught by Mohammad, who, cross at being interrupted, spoke roughly to him. But his conscience quickly smote him for his harshness, and the next day's Revelation reproved him. It is thus given in the Korân.

> 'He frowned, and he turned his back,
> Because the blind man came to him!
> But what assured thee that he would not
> Be cleansed by the Faith,
> Or be warned and the warning profit him?
> As to him who is wealthy,
> To him thou wast all attention;
> Yet is it not thy concern if he be not cleansed:
> But as to him who cometh to thee in earnest,
> And full of fears—him dost thou neglect.'

Mohammad afterwards sought the man, saying, 'He is thrice welcome on whose account my Lord hath reprimanded me.'

He began to teach abroad in Mecca and other places, but the attacks on him grew so bitter, that he had to leave the city. On his return his wife died. She was a true and noble-natured woman and her memory is held in deep reverence, visits being paid to her tomb every Friday. To add to Mohammad's troubles, poverty came upon him, and a plot being laid to kill him, he had to leave Mecca a second time, and started for Medina, where some of his converts lived. On his way thither he and a friend hid in a cave, over the mouth of which a spider spun its web as they lay inside. When their pursuers came to the cave they felt sure, on seeing the web, that Mohammad was not there. 'We are but two,' said his friend, full of fear. 'There is a third,' replied Mohammad, 'it is God Himself.'

The Muslims date their years from the prophet's flight to Medina, just as we date history from the birth of Jesus Christ. On reaching that city, all was changed. A glad welcome greeted Mohammad and he at once became ruler and lawgiver.

But he ceased to be only the preacher of a creed beautiful and simple, and became a warrior.

He was angered against those who had refused to believe in him and, since he could not persuade them, he sought to compel them. So he offered idolaters and Jews either death or conversion to Islám, and urged his followers to battle by promising immediate entrance into Paradise to those who fell in the fight. They flung themselves without fear into the contest, for to them it was God's battle against the unfaithful, and Islám! His will be done.

Mohammad's anger was hottest against the Jews. He had striven hard to win them to his side. He admitted their religion to be divine; he adopted many of their rites and doctrines and made Jerusalem the Kiblah or place toward which men were to turn in daily prayer. But they ridiculed him and cut him to the quick with satire and sneer, so that to the day of his death he was their bitter foe. The Sabbath was changed to Friday, which was the day when the Arabs were used to meet in assembly, and Muslims were commanded to turn their faces toward Mecca. After wars against Arabs, Jews and Christians, in the greater number of which Mohammad was the victor, he had conquered the whole of Arabia and extended his rule to other parts. So great had his power become that he sent messages to kings and princes demanding that they would submit to Islám.

Towards the tenth year after his flight, he went on his last pilgrimage to Mecca at the head of 40,000 Muslims. On his return to Medina, feeling death near, he dwelt near the mosque that he might take part as long as he could in the public prayers. After calling the people together he asked them, as did Samuel when he bade farewell to the children of Israel, 'whether he had wronged anyone or whether he owed aught to anyone' and then after reading some verses from the Korân, went home to die. He passed away in his sixty-second year amidst the deep grief of the people, and a great tumult arose at the news, for many thought him immortal.

He was a great and true man, and the religion which he set forth met the needs of men in the East as no other religion did in that day, nor is it likely that it will ever cease its hold upon men or that Mohammad will give place to any other prophet.

We must no more blame him for many of the sad errors and vices mixed up with Islám than we should blame Jesus for the evils which have crept into Christianity. Even for the wars that he waged he may have found excuse in the history of the Jews. The Old Testament is reddened, in its books of their history, with the story of the shameful cruelty of which they were guilty, of tender children slaughtered, of whole cities put to the edge of the sword, and all this butchery done, as they would have us believe, in the name and at the command of the Lord, of Whom their ideas were so gross that they more than once offered human sacrifices to Him. And we all know what terrible wars and massacres have taken place in the name of our Christian religion, and how but a very few years ago it was held by many Christians that man could own and buy and sell his fellow-man.

Brighter and better days have come since then, and Mohammadans, like Christians, do not now seek to spread their faith by violence and bloodshed. I have dwelt upon this because it is needful to see how little of the grosser part of each religion belongs, in most cases, to the idea of its founder.

In addition to what has been said about Islám, Muslims believe that God in different ages made known His will to prophets in scriptures, of which all but four are lost; the Pentateuch (or first five books of the Bible), the Psalms, the Gospel, and the Korân; the Korân only being perfect. Also that there will be, after many strange events, a resurrection and a final judgment, when the souls of both the good and bad will have to pass over a bridge laid across hell, finer than a hair and sharper than a sword. The souls of the good will pass quickly across it, but the wicked will fall into hell headlong. The idea of heaven is that of a place of gross delights; while a never-ending hell will be the fate of all non-believers.

The success of Islám was great. Not 100 years after the death of the prophet, it had converted half the then known world, and its green flag waved from China to Spain. Christianity gave way before it, and has never regained some of the ground then lost, while at this day we see Islám making marked progress in Africa and elsewhere. Travellers tell us that the gain is great when a tribe casts away its idols and embraces Islám. Filth and drunkenness flee away, and the state of the people is bettered in a high degree.

When we hear good-meaning people lament that negroes should become Mohammadans, let us remember that this was not the feeling of Jesus when his disciples told him that they had forbidden a man who was casting out demons in his name. 'And Jesus said, Forbid him not: for he that is not against us is for us.' And this, I am sure, he would say to-day of the Mohammadan missionaries, if he were amongst us.

Along the northern coasts of Africa and nearly to the equator, from Turkey to within the borders of China, and among the larger islands of the East, the faith of Islám spreads, divided into sects, and numbers millions who offer to Allâh their five-fold daily prayer. From every mosque the blind mueddin or crier proclaims at daybreak ; 'There is no God but God ; Mohammad is His prophet. Prayer is better than sleep ; come to prayer,' and then each pious Muslim falls facewards to the holy city Mecca.

I should add that the wars of Islám did not leave waste and ruin in their path, but that the Arabs, when they came to Europe, alone held aloft the light of learning, and in the once famous schools of Spain, taught 'philosophy, medicine, astronomy, and the golden art of song.' The Arabic words used in science—*algebra, almanack, alcohol,* and others, together with many names of stars, remain among us as proofs of what Arabia has given to Europe.

The Mohammadan Bible is the Kuran or Korân. *Al-Korân* or *The Reading* (as we say; *The Bible*) contains the entire code of Islám; that is, it is not a book of religious precepts merely, but it governs all that a Muslim does.

I shall not waste limited space in giving the absurd story which the Muslims tell about their Korân, but briefly speak of its contents. It is entirely the work of Mohammad, and is made up of revelations which he believed came to him from the time of his sojourn on Mount Hira. It is regarded not only as inspired every word, but as uncreated and eternal. It consists of 114 Súrahs or chapters, which were dictated by Mohammad to a scribe, and the copies thus made were thrown into a box. A year after Mohammad's death, such portions as remained were collected 'from date-leaves, tablets of white stone, bones, parchment-leaves,' and memories of men, and copied without order of time or subject, the longest chapters being put first.

The titles of the chapters are taken from some chief matter in them, but are mostly unmeaning, affording no clue to the contents, as for example, 'The Cow;' 'Thunder;' 'The Fig;' 'The Elephant.' Each begins with the words, 'In the name of God, the Compassionate, the Merciful,' and also tells where it was revealed to Mohammad.

The Korân is written in the purest and most elegant Arabic, and suffers much by translation. Teaching the oneness of God, it is largely made up of stories, legends, laws and counsels which show how much use Mohammad made of all that he had heard of Jewish history and lore.

Much of it, as we read it, seems utterly unmeaning, other parts of it move us by the beauty of their desert songs of God's majesty and purity.

The Muslims do not touch it with unwashed hands, and never hold it below the girdle round their waist, while to them nothing is more hateful than to see it in the hands of an unbeliever.

They regard this short chapter as equal to one-third of the whole book in value:

> 'Say there is one God alone—
> God the eternal;
> He begetteth not and He is not begotten,
> And there is none like unto him.'

I have marked many Súrahs with the view of quoting from them, but can give only three or four specimens.

This Súrah, named 'the folding up,' thus describes the last day:

'When the sun shall be folded up,
And when the stars shall fall,
And when the mountains shall be set in motion,
And when the she-camels with young shall be neglected,
And when the wild beasts shall be huddled together,
And when the seas shall boil,
And when the souls shall be joined again to their bodies,

And when the leaves of the Book shall be unrolled,
And when the heavens shall be stripped away like a skin,
And when hell shall be made to blaze,
And when paradise shall be brought near,
Every soul shall know what it has done.'

At the end of another Súrah, and one of the latest in point of time, this fine passage occurs:

'God! there is no God but He, the Living, the Eternal. Slumber doth not overtake Him, neither sleep; to Him belongeth all that is in heaven and earth. Who is he that can plead with Him but by His own permission? He knoweth that which is past, and that which is to come unto them, and they shall not comprehend anything of His knowledge but so far as he pleaseth. His throne is extended over heaven and earth, and the upholding of both is no burden unto Him. He is the Lofty and Great.'

Again:

'It is God who hath ordained the night for your rest, and the day to give you light: verily God is rich in bounties to most men; but most men render not the tribute of thanks.

'This is God your Lord, Creator of all things; no god is there but He: why then do ye turn away from Him?

Again:

'O my son! observe prayer, and enjoin the right and forbid the wrong, and be patient under whatever shall betide thee: for this is a bounden duty. And distort not thy face at men; nor walk thou loftily on the earth; for God loveth no arrogant vain-glorious one.

'But let thy pace be middling; and lower thy voice; for the least pleasing of voices is surely the voice of asses.'

And as a last quotation:

'There is no piety in turning your faces towards the east or the west, but he is pious who believeth in God, and the last day, and the angels, and the scriptures, and the prophets; who for the love of God disburseth his wealth to his kindred, and to the orphans, and to the needy, and the wayfarer, and those who ask, and for ransoming; who observeth prayer, and payeth the legal alms, and who is of those who are faithful to their engagements when they have engaged in them, and patient under ills and hardships, and in time of trouble; these are they who are just, and these are they who fear the Lord.'

CHAPTER XIII.

ON THE STUDY OF THE BIBLE.

IN the remarks which were made on the right use of legends of the past, I promised to show you why the Bible should be read as we read other books. It is a common notion that the Bible has to be treated in some different way; and owing to that chiefly, it is, although one of the most read, yet the most misread of books and the least understood. The care which has to be applied, the free, full use of the powers of the mind which has to be made to enable us to get at the meaning of any book, is often most strangely withheld by people when reading the Bible.

The fact has already come before you that there are several book-religions in the world, and this will have caused you to ask in what way the book on which our Christian religion is founded differs from the books on which other religions are founded. For it is clear that what Christians believe concerning the Bible, namely, that it is the work of men specially helped by God, Who made use of them to reveal truths needful for us to know and which none of us could ever have found out for himself, and that it is free from the errors and defects which every other book contains; is believed in a still more intense degree by the Brahmans concerning the Veda, by the Muslims concerning the Korân, and so on.

The knowledge of this renders it needful for us to enquire whether our belief is ill or well grounded, whether we have surer proof of its truth than the Brahman has of his, for to neglect this is to confess that we shrink from comparing the Bible with the Veda, fearful lest it might suffer thereby, and the grand truths which it contains become less dear to us.

There are plenty of books within reach which give an account of the contents of the Bible, of the order in which the books which compose it are believed to have been written, of the supposed dates and places, of the names of the authors, and like matters relating to its wonderful history. All these may here be passed by and give place to a few simple facts which are more or less known, but which are much overlooked, and upon which all proof as to the value of the Bible must ever rest.

The first of these is that the Bible was produced like every book; *men wrote it.* It is made up of a number of works of the most varied kind; history, poem, proverb, prophecy, epistle; all written by learned or unlearned men, many of them unknown to one another, since they lived in different lands and centuries apart; each as he wrote his history or poured forth his song little thinking that it would form part of a book which has been precious to millions of men for hundreds of years, which 'goes equally to the cottage of the plain man and the palace of the king; which is woven into the literature of the scholar and colours the talk of the street; which mingles in all the grief and cheerfulness of life; which blesses us when we are born; gives names to half Christendom; rejoices with us; has sympathy for our mourning;' a book, every portion of which, strange to say, has been regarded as of equal value; whether it be the Book of Esther or the Epistle to the Romans.

And not only did men write it; *men also collected its books together.* The books of the Old Testament were gathered together by the Jews, when or by whom among them is not known That ancient people guarded them with jealous care, using all pains to prevent errors entering into the copies which were made, every verse and letter being counted.

The books of the New Testament were chosen from many others and assumed their present form about the end of the second century after Christ, but men and churches have differed much and still differ as to which books should be left out and which admitted.

Not only did men write the several books of the Bible and collect them into one volume: *men also translated them* into our own and other languages, doing, in the case of our translation, a great and noble work, filled with the richness, simplicity and power of our sweet mother-tongue, before cramped and stilted words of Latin birth were brought into it. But grand and lasting as their workmanship was, our translators made many mistakes, some of them wilful ones, (as, for example, when, in their rarely printed 'Preface to the Reader,' they say that they have made use of certain words by the express command of the king), which a body of learned men of our day are now busily employed in correcting. Then the division of the books of Scripture into chapters and verses, some of these, as where Genesis ii. 1-3 is severed from Genesis i., being wrong; and the headings to the chapters, some of which give a false idea of their contents, was each the work of men. The words printed in italics are not in the manuscripts which were translated, but were added by our translators to complete the sense, although in some cases they obscure it.

Now no one asserts that the men who *collected* the books together were inspired by God to do it, so that they could not by any means leave out the right books and put in the wrong books, nor that the men who *translated* the Bible were inspired, so that they could not give a wrong meaning to the Greek or Hebrew in turning it into our own or any other tongue. We must therefore put these on one side and pass to the men who wrote the books, and who, it is commonly believed, were inspired by God to do it, and preserved from all error in their work.

Various opinions are held about the nature and extent of this inspiration, some few believing that every word, every syllable and every letter is the direct utterance of God; others, that the writers were kept from error when revealing His will, but not when speaking upon matters of history, science, &c. All debate about this is in vain, because if any manuscripts ever existed, which were the work of men thus helped, we have no true copies of them, since the oldest manuscripts differ in important details. And even if the very handiwork of each writer could be found, the belief that he was inspired would in no way help us to understand what he had written. But it is said the Bible writers claim to speak the very words of God, and it is this which makes it so needful for us to listen to them with obedient heart and trustful soul. Of course such a claim, like the claims of certain men in past and present days to power to forgive sins, is more easily made than proven, and all we can do is to go to the Bible itself and see what is therein said and how far it supports the claim.

The frequent use in the Old Testament of such solemn phrases as 'Thus saith the Lord;' 'And God said;' 'God spake these words and said;' the verses which tell us that 'All scripture is given by inspiration of God;' that 'holy men of old spake as they were moved by the Holy Ghost,' form the chief foundation on which the claim is rested.

Upon the use of the phrases quoted, some very instructive facts are given by Sir Samuel Baker in his book on the 'Nile Tributaries.' He says (pp. 129-131) 'the conversation of the Arabs is in the exact style of the Old Testament. The name of God is coupled with every trifling incident in life. Should a famine afflict the country, it is expressed in the stern language of the Old Testament: "The Lord has sent a grievous famine upon the land," or "The Lord called for a famine and it came upon the land." Should their cattle fall sick, it is considered to be an affliction by divine command; or should the flocks prosper and multiply, the prosperity is attributed to divine interference. . . . . This striking likeness to the descriptions of the Old Testament is most interesting to a traveller when living among these people. With the Bible in one hand, and these unchanged tribes before the eyes, there is a thrilling illustration of the sacred records; the past becomes the present; the veil of 3000 years is raised, and the living picture is a witness to the exactness of the historical description. At the same time there is a light thrown upon many obscure passages in the Old Testament by the experience of the present customs and figures of speech of the Arabs; which are exactly like those that were practised at the periods described. . . . Should the present history of the country be written by an Arab scribe, the style of the description would be purely that of the Old Testament, and the various calamities, or the good fortunes that have, in the course of nature, befallen both the tribes and individuals would be recounted either as special visitations of divine wrath or blessings for good deeds performed. If in a dream a particular course of action is suggested, the Arab believes that God has *spoken* and directed him. The Arab scribe or historian would describe the event as the "*voice* of the

Lord" having spoken unto the person; or that God appeared to him in a dream, and "*said,*" &c. Thus much allowance would be necessary on the part of a European reader for the figurative ideas and expressions of the people.'

When we go to the Bible, we find therein exactly what those who have some knowledge of its wonderful history might expect. It bears the traces of the long years through which it was slowly growing, book by book. In its earlier pages we find legends which, as already shown, are very like to those of nations with whom the Jew were connected by race or came in contact; we find there ideas about God which are coarse and degrading, which became lofty only as the Jews advanced in the thought of Him as pictured in the worthy language of the prophets, and which were altogether different from the ennobling teaching of Jesus and of Paul; we find how deeply human all its writers were; how each differs in his style of telling anything and is marked by it; how fully they shared the common beliefs of their time; nor is it easy to find in what they have said truths which, in one form or another, have not been stated by the writers of some of the sacred books into which we have dipped.

The Bible records the experience of the wisest and best of men of the past in their search after truth, but it is hard to discover proof that the claim to inspiration which is made for them, and which they would perhaps not claim for themselves, is one that cannot be denied. And if it be admitted, the inspiration would be without value unless it was also bestowed upon the men who copied the manuscripts, upon the men who collected them together, upon the men who translated them, and in short, upon every one who in any way has had to do with placing the Bible in the hands of people of any age and clime.

It may appear a graceless thing to write any words which shall seem to lessen the value of a book which for hundreds of years has been so precious to men. But the loss is more seeming than real, since riddance of error leaves room for truth to enter, and it is far better to be quit of false notions in early life than to undergo the painful and weary task of uprooting them in after years.

The truths which are enshrined in the Bible are not less true because frail men spake them, nor is that, 'inspiration of the Almighty' which 'giveth understanding' a less mighty fact because we find that the writers of Scripture had it not different in kind to that which comes to every man who opens his soul to receive it. It dwelt in those earnest ones whose yearnings after the unseen found utterance in Bible, Rig-Veda, Zend-Avesta, Tripitaka, King and Korân, and it dwells in earnest souls to-day, wherever the love of truth abides. And for us, in whatever written or spoken word, or sound of many-voiced nature, we find that which speaks to our heart **as true,** *there* **is for us an inspired truth.**

CONCLUSION.

This outline sketch would have been more complete if an account had been given of some religions that have passed away, but of which fragments remain here and there in hoary rite and custom.

For example, there was the religion of EGYPT, land of marvel and of mystery: fountain of knowledge at which Assyrian, Greek and Hebrew drank; noted for its discoveries in science, and for the majesty, and withal the delicacy, of its art; for the highly civilized state of its people, whose daily life — the luxury and pleasures of the few — the toil and hardship of the many — is pictured on wall-paintings, preserved from decay by a rainless climate through five thousand years. That religion, standing in awe before the mystery of life, looked upon all life as divine, and had its upper gods of Nature, Space and Time; its sun and river deities; its worship of insect, bird, reptile and beast chiefest of which was the Apis bull of Memphis; its belief in an immortal life, and a judgment after death, of which the proofs are near us in the mummies of animals and human beings, and in the great sacred book known as the 'Ritual of the Dead.' Behind the forms of that religion in pompous festivals, minute ceremonies, sacrifices, charms, and months and days each dedicate to the gods, there were secrets which the priests kept to themselves, through which the religion became a priestcraft.

There was the religion of GREECE, revelling in sunlight and gladness; its gods most strong and goddesses most fair, dwelling on Mount Olympus, were beings not free from the follies and vices of men, for they spent their lives in fighting, feasting, scheming and love-making. Ruling mankind, they were in their turn ruled by Fate, and therefore inspired neither fear nor respect. In the Greek religion the beautiful was the divine, and he was accounted most godlike who added by his art to all that pleased the eye, or that fell musically upon the ear. Lovely forms filled every nook and corner of that sunny land: the echoes of the nymphs' soft voices were heard among the mountains, they dwelt within the forest-trees, and slept beside the streams. There was no priestly caste, for to pray and sacrifice was the right of every free-born Greek; there were no sacred books, but deep reverence for the poet's words. Rich feasts and festivals, mysteries and oracles, entered largely into the Greek religion, but the cheerfulness of this life did not lend itself to colour the ideas of a life to come, which were dim and misty.

There was the religion of ROME, empire once splendid and stately beyond compare; a religion with no lustre in its eye, no life in its heart, if heart it had, but as loveless a thing as the soul whom Tennyson so wonderfully describes in his 'Palace of Art.' It was a worship of law and duty, neither of which we should leave undone, but it was not an obedience to law and a loyalty to duty springing out of love. It was given to the gods as their due, as a man pays his just debts. There were gods many, Jupiter being the chief, and under him deities representing the powers of nature, or ruling over money, trade, the house, &c., and a goodly number had been borrowed from Greece, but they left their souls behind them. A long list of festivals filled the year, and song and dance entered into the honours paid the gods, but the true object of worship among the Romans was Rome. That a higher life beat within the souls of some is proved by the noble thoughts of Seneca, Marcus Aurelius, and others, which have come down to us.

There was the religion of the TEUTONS and Scandinavians, whose blood is in our veins. Its gods, huge, shaggy giants, took shape and character from the wild, bleak regions of the north. Their virtue was their strength and courage, and their work an unending fight against storm and snow and darkness. And as with the gods, so with the men. To them life was an earnest thing, war its business, bravery its duty, cowardice its greatest crime. To escape death in bed, since for those thus dying Hela waited in her cold prison-house below, where hunger was her dish, starvation her knife, care her bed, and anguish its curtains; men would be carried into battle, or mimic a violent death by cutting wounds in their flesh, that Odin's Choosers of the Slain might lead them to his hall (Valhalla), where they fought at dawn, and if wounded, were healed by noon, ready for the feast and song. There was withal tenderness and warmth within these rough Norsemen's hearts, and when they gave up beautiful Baldur, son of Odin, for Jesus, son of God, the missionaries of the cross gained their noblest triumph.

In brief, the Egyptians worshipped *nature;* the Greeks, *beauty;* the Romans, *law;* and the Northern races, *courage.*

Then there were the religions of Babylon, Phœnicia, and other mighty nations; of the Aztecs of Mexico and the Incas of Peru; and there is a valuable field of study in learning about the beliefs and practices existing among the tribes of Africa, America, Polynesia, &c., since they furnish illustrations of those earliest forms of religion out of which have slowly risen the ennobling beliefs of the most advanced races of mankind.

But all this, and very much more, must be passed by.

There is, however, one question which makes itself heard in many parts of this book and to which an answer must be given. It is this: How do the facts brought together herein about the great religions of the world bear on our Christian religion, and what is the relation between them and it? To worthily answer this would fill many pages, and it must suffice to give one or two reasons for replying that our religion, while beyond question the highest of all, takes a place not distinct from, but among all religions, past or present. Its relation to them is not that they are earthborn, while it alone is divine, but it is the relation of one member of a family to other members, who are 'all brothers, having one work, one hope and one All-Father.'

I know that it is not always easy to think thus of it, because it is dear to us as no other religion ever could be, linked as it is by love towards him who lived the saintliest life and died the martyr-death, and in following whose example we follow all that is beautiful and divine. But viewing it as one amongst others, much that otherwise perplexes and even dismays us is taken away, and we cease to wonder that its history is so like that of other religions. We are able to understand why it has grown from small beginnings and been subject to many changes, as they have, if we believe that it also had its rise in the nature of man. We understand how the early disciples of Jesus treasured with loving care the memory of what he had said, and how, as the years rolled on, it seemed good to some of them to commit what they knew or had heard to writings which in course of time took shape as the New Testament. We see how the simple faith of the first Christians became sadly corrupted, how word-mongers and creed-makers stifled it, how, petted in kingly courts and clad in earthly armour, its kingdom became of this world. We read of its victories and defeats; its divisions and their brood of hate, cruelty and martyrdom; its failure to regain some of the ground lost and to win to itself races whose religions were grey with age when it was born. And we read too, how, in the good providence of God, it was embraced by the nations descended from those Aryan tribes who travelled into Europe and to whom He has given so great a part to play in this world's rough story; and how, by that love of man which is its life, it made helpful to the world's good those mighty forces to which it was thus joined.

All this, and very much more that could be added, becomes clear as the noonday if Christianity be regarded as like in kind to other faiths; while treated as altogether unlike, its slow progress and varying fortunes bewilder us, and our trust grows feeble and perishes.

I have said thus much, because neither you nor I are likely to give up our religion and become Muslims or Buddhists, and also because I would have you without fear compare it with theirs, and gladly welcome in each that which we know is common to all, and which makes us 'all brothers, because we have one work and one hope and one All-Father.'

I have been more careful to collect facts relating to the matter of this book than to ask what they mean, since in every study the mastery of facts and the knowledge of their relation to one another is of the first importance. Conclusions can always wait and always take care of themselves. But now that the end of our story is reached, I must say a few words suggested by what it tells.

1. In all things we see purpose and progress.

No race of people has been placed where it is found by chance, for God hath appointed the bounds of its habitation, and when it moves, it is His hand that guides it towards 'one far-off, divine event.'

Deep down in the earth's crust there are remains of the dim specks of life from which have come forms of life higher and still higher, till the lordliest and the best appeared.

The lichens that rest 'starlike on the stone' and tree-trunk, that, with the mosses, cover the wide moorlands and adorn the mountain-side where nought else will grow, these prepare a soil into which the noblest trees of the forest can strike their roots.

The caves and old river-beds disclose the rough stone tools which the common sense of savage man shaped to point and edge, and by the use of which he made possible that which we are to-day in this Age of Iron. And it is the same with man's higher nature. First cringing, awe-struck, before some misshapen stone, or before the dead yet moving powers in cloud and river, then worshipping living creatures, and so on step by step until, with now a stumble and now a fall, he rises from worship of the thing made to worship of its Maker; from reverence, born of fear, for the *strong*, to adoration, born of love, for the *holy*. Every morning there steal up the eastern sky the early rays that gently prepare our waking eyes for the brighter light of the sun, whose glory would dazzle if it burst upon us suddenly, and in like manner, in the dawn of this world's history, God let truth into the minds of men little by little, yet ever pouring forth more as they were able to receive it, and still it increases and will increase, shining 'more and more unto the perfect day.'

2. What has been said pre-supposes the fact that man is a religious being.

Look where we will, we find that when his bodily wants, be they few or many, have been supplied, there remains a craving which no gift of earth can satisfy, the craving of his heart after God. All men have it, although in some it sleeps, and it is the same in all none the less because it shows itself in different ways. Under various forms we see expressed a sense of need; a belief as in the *savage*, in a will *mightier* than his own;

as in the *civilized* man, in a will *holier* than his own; a feeling of duty which, in the lowest races, takes what is to us a brutal shape, but which is none the less such a feeling; as, for example, when the Feejee kills his aged parent under the fear that he may become too feeble to undertake the journey to another world; and lastly, the universal belief that a man's soul or self does not die, but haunts the place it lived in, or betakes itself to some far-off happy land.

Such being the nature of man, we must be careful lest we speak or think meanly of him and thus dishonour his Creator. He who has a low and unworthy idea of his nature will act unworthily; while he who feels how great is the life of a being made in the image of God will not readily blot and blur that image. If anyone be told that he cannot choose the right and love the true, and live out the pure, he will feel that if it be so, to try is hopeless work. But we are very sure that it is not so, else how could there dwell within us sorrow and unquiet after doing wrong, if we did not feel that we can do, and ought to do the right? If such chilling unfaith in themselves and in their kind had been in the heart of the saintly men whose lives have blessed the world; who, like salt, have kept the mass from decay; how, think you, could they have dared and done? They had faith in man as the fruit of faith in the God who made him; they felt that the life of man is not what it will one day become, and this it was that fired them to earnest effort in the service and salvation of their fellows, and to help on the time when earth shall be the paradise it never has been yet:

> 'Who rowing hard against the stream,
> Saw distant gates of Eden gleam,
> And did not dream it was a dream.'

It is the faith of such men, some of whose lives have been looked at in this book, that you and I must share. Life is full of duty, and to do well the work that lies close at hand is to fulfil the purpose for which we were sent here. The weakest and youngest amongst us is a power for good as well as for evil, and it should be our aim to do our part on the side of ever-increasing human goodness against ever-lessening human badness:

CONCLUSION.

There is but one life, if life it may be called, which seems to me to be God-forsaken; it is the life that is idle or selfish. Those few words express more than one might think, but their meaning has been set to sweeter music than I can command by Leigh Hunt in the story of Abou Ben Adhem, with which I close this book:

> 'Abou Ben Adhem—may his tribe increase!—
> Awoke one night from a deep dream of peace,
> And saw amid the moonlight in his room,
> Making it rich, and like a lily in bloom,
> An angel writing in a book of gold;
> Exceeding peace had made Ben Adhem bold,
> And to the vision in the room he said,
> "What writest thou?" The vision raised its head,
> And with a voice made of all sweet accord,
> Replied, "The names of them that love the Lord."
> "And is mine one?" said Abou. "Nay, not so,"
> Replied the angel. Abou spoke more low,
> But cheerly still, and said, "I pray thee, then,
> "Write me as one who loves his fellow men."
>
> The angel wrote and vanished. The next night
> He came again with a great wakening light;
> He showed the names whom love of God had blest,
> And lo! Ben Adhem's name led all the rest.'

APPENDIX.

NOTE A, page 22.

ON THE LIKENESS BETWEEN CERTAIN CHALDEAN AND JEWISH LEGENDS.

The resemblance between some of these legends has been shown at pp. 22, 71, but the most remarkable and interesting illustration appears while this book is passing through the press. Among the tablets brought from Assyria by Mr George Smith, who, it will be remembered, was first sent there at the expense of the spirited proprietors of the *Daily Telegraph*, are a series of fragments which, joined to some smaller pieces in the British Museum collection, give 'the history of the world from the Creation down to some period after the fall of man.' Pending the issue of a promised full translation of the legends, which will be eagerly awaited, their accomplished and unwearying discoverer has announced his success in a letter to the *Daily Telegraph*, 4th March 1875, wherein he gives the following brief account of the contents of the tablets:

'Whatever the primitive account may have been from which the earlier part of the Book of Genesis was copied, it is evident that the brief narration given in the Pentateuch omits a number of incidents and explanations—for instance, as to the origin of evil, the fall of the angels, the wickedness of the serpent, &c. Such points as these are included in the

Cuneiform narrative; but of course I can say little about them until I prepare full translations of the legends.

'The narrative on the Assyrian tablets commences with a description of the period before the world was created, when there existed a chaos or confusion. The desolate and empty state of the universe and the generation by chaos of monsters are vividly given. The chaos is presided over by a female power named Tisalat and Tiamat, corresponding to the Thalatth of Berosus; but as it proceeds the Assyrian account agrees rather with the Bible than with the short account from Berosus. We are told, in the inscriptions, of the fall of the celestial being who appears to correspond to Satan. In his ambition he raises his hand against the sanctuary of the God of heaven, and the description of him is really magnificent. He is represented riding in a chariot through celestial space, surrounded by the storms, with the lightning playing before him, and wielding a thunderbolt as a weapon.

'This rebellion leads to a war in heaven and the conquest of the powers of evil, the gods in due course creating the universe in stages, as in the Mosaic narrative, surveying each step of the work and pronouncing it good. The divine work culminates in the creation of man, who is made upright and free from evil, and endowed by the gods with the noble faculty of speech.

'The Deity then delivers a long address to the newly-created being, instructing him in all his duties and privileges, and pointing out the glory of his state. But this condition of blessing does not last long before man, yielding to temptation, falls; and the Deity then pronounces upon him a terrible curse, invoking on his head all the evils which have since afflicted humanity. These last details are, as I have before stated, upon the fragment which I excavated during my first journey to Assyria. and the discovery of this single relic in my opinion increases many times over the value of *The Daily Telegraph* collection.

'I have at present recovered no more of the story, and am not yet in a position to give the full translations and details; but I hope during the spring to find time to search over the collection of smaller fragments of tablets, and to light upon any smaller parts of the legends which may have escaped me. There will arise, besides, a number of important questions as to the date and origin of the legends, their comparison with the Biblical narrative, and as to how far they may supplement the Mosaic account.'

In a valuable contribution to the *Academy*, 20th March 1875, Mr Sayce shows that the Phœnician legends form, as it were, the link between the Chaldean and the Hebrew so far as the so-called Elohistic portion of Genesis is concerned: this being especially noticeable in the legend of the Creation and the sacrifice of Isaac (upon which cf. Haug's 'Aitareya-Brâhmana;' Max Müller's Anct. Sans. Lit. 408-17; Gubernati's Zool. Mythol., I. 69; and the Greek myth of Agamemnon and Iphigenia). Mr Sayce also explains the very close resemblance between the Babylonian and Jewish legends of the garden of Eden, the Deluge, and the Tower of Babel, the Phœnician analogies failing us here altogether. But the whole subject is still in its infancy, and, as Prof. de Gubernati remarks, "when we shall be able to bring into Semitic studies the same liberty of scientific criticism which is conceded to Aryan studies, we shall have a Semitic mythology; for the present, faith, a natural sense of repugnance to abandon the beloved superstitions of our credulous childhood, and more than all, a less honourable sentiment of terror for the opinion of the world, have restrained men of study from examining Jewish history and tradition with entire impartiality and severity of judgment.' *(Vol. II. 410, 412.)*

NOTE B, page 31.

ON THE ORIGIN OF THE SOLAR SYSTEM.

In endeavouring to give a clear and untechnical account of Laplace's nebular hypothesis so that its main features may be comprehended by young persons, I have not thought it desirable to introduce any remarks upon the insufficiency of that hypothesis to explain the arrangement of the varying masses of the major and minor planets of our system. My friend Mr Proctor, with his accustomed clearness and independent examination of all hypotheses, has, I think, shown conclusively that 'a theory involving combined processes of accretion and contraction is the true hypothesis of the evolution of the solar system.' (See his works generally, but especially 'Other Worlds than Ours,' pp. 210-19, and an article on 'The Past and Future of our Earth,' *Contemp. Rev.*, Dec. 1874.) The accretion, due to the indrawing of matter from the infinite space around, falls in with all that we have learnt of the intimate relation between every system of every galaxy composing a universe wherein neither sun nor minutest atom dwells in isolation.

Subject to the modification thus indicated, all our present knowledge points to nebular condensation as the origin of suns with their systems. That vast masses of matter exist in a gaseous and highly incandescent state is proved by the spectroscope. That such masses are cooling by radiation, with the inevitable result of condensation and rotation is equally certain; and if the result of the observations of Mr Ellery and others, now extending over a period of some years, upon the nebula surrounding the star Eta Argûs in the southern hemisphere may be relied upon, then such a process is going on under the eyes of the astronomers of to-day. (See

Monthly Notices of the Royal Astronomical Society, xxv. p. 192; xxviii. pp. 200, 225; xxix. p. 82; xxxiv. p. 269.)

NOTE C, page 50.

ON THE PUNISHMENT OF ANIMALS AND LIFELESS OBJECTS AS THE CAUSE OF INJURY TO MANKIND.

The belief entertained by man in the myth-making stage of his progress that all motion in things around is actuated by personal life and will analogous to his own, and differing only in degree, goes far to explain why even inanimate objects have been held criminally responsible for disaster occasioned by them. Commenting upon the mental condition which causes the savage to bite the stone over which he stumbles and the civilized man to kick the chair against which he bruises himself, Dr Tylor remarks in his 'Primitive Culture,' Vol. I. 259, that it 'may be traced along the course of history, not merely in impulsive habit, but in formally enacted law. The rude Kukis of Southern Asia were very scrupulous in carrying out their simple law of vengeance, life for life; if a tiger killed a Kuki, his family were in disgrace till they had retaliated by killing and eating this tiger, or another; but further, if a man was killed by a fall from a tree, his relatives would take their revenge by cutting the tree down and scattering it in chips. A modern king of Cochin China, when one of his ships sailed badly, used to put it in the pillory as he would any other criminal. In classical times the stories of Xerxes flogging the Hellespont and Cyrus draining the Gyndes occur as cases in point, but one of the regular Athenian legal proceedings is a yet more striking relic. A court of justice was held at the Prytaneum, to try any inanimate object, such as an axe or a piece of wood or stone which had caused the death of any one without proved human agency, and this wood or stone, if condemned, was in solemn form cast beyond the border (Grote, iii. p. 104; v. p. 22). The spirit of this remarkable procedure reappears in the old English law (repealed in the present reign in 1846), whereby not only a beast that kills a man, but a cart-wheel that runs over him, or a tree that falls on him and kills him, is deodand or given to God, *i.e.*, forfeited and sold for the poor : as Bracton says, "Omnia quæ movent ad mortem sunt Deodanda."' And among the records of ancient legislation in France upon similar matters, we have, on the 4th June 1094, the hanging of a pig for devouring the babe of a cowherd at Laon, and twenty-six years later the excommunication by the Bishop of Laon of a swarm of caterpillars; while 'in 1516, the Courts of Troyes, complying with the prayers of the inhabitants of Villenoxe, admonished the caterpillars by which that district was then infested to take themselves off within six days, on pain of being declared "accursed and excommunicated!"' A sanction for the punishment of animals would be found in the Jewish law, which directed that 'if an ox gore a man or woman that they die; then the ox shall be surely stoned and his flesh shall not be eaten.' (Exodus xxi. 28; Cf. also Genesis ix. 5.)

NOTE D, page 53.

ON THE SUPPOSED BIRTHPLACE OF MANKIND.

Although the old notions as to the recent advent of man upon this planet are refuted by the evidence now accumulated as to his immense antiquity, it is true that he is relatively modern when compared with the creatures that preceded him, while the further back that we push the geological epoch of his appearance, even to the Miocene period, the more cumulative is the evidence in favour of the unity of origin of the various races. But when we endeavour to fix upon the site of the original home of mankind, the evidence at hand is so slight that it behoves us to speak with the utmost caution. Looking to man's slender organization, and to the absence of any natural protection against cold, it seems probable that he arose in some warm region, and in remarking that such region may have been a land now submerged beneath the Indian Ocean, to which Professor Sclater has given the appropriate name 'Lemuria,' we have the assertion of Professor Huxley that the geographical distribution of the Negro race cannot be explained except on the hypothesis that great changes have occurred since the appearance of that race, changes involving the submersion of an immense tract of land, or closely-linked chain of islands stretching eastwards from Africa. (Cf. Huxley on 'The Methods and Results of Ethnology,' *Fortnightly Review*, i. pp. 257 *et seq.*; Lubbock's 'Pre-Historic Times,' pp. 387, 388, 3d edit.) In a review of Dr Peschel's 'Ethnology' (Völkerkunde), of which valuable work a translation is announced as forthcoming, Dr Tylor, in commenting on the theory that 'Lemuria' was the cradle of mankind, remarks as follows —'Such a continent, Dr Peschel thinks, is an anthropological necessity for Australians, Coolies, Papuans and Negroes, to reach their present homes almost dry-shod. As to climate, moreover, this birthplace of man would be situated in the very zone of the anthropoid apes. It is remarked that such a choice of the region of man's first appearance would be more orthodox than seems at first sight, for here we are in the neighbourhood of the four mysterious rivers of Eden, namely, the Nile, Euphrates, Tigris and Indus. And in the gradual submergence of Lemuria we see pitilessly accomplished the expulsion from Paradise, situated, as the old geographers knew, in south-east Asia. This, Dr Peschel is careful to add, is only an hypothesis, but it is an hypothesis which may lead to geological investigations of Madagascar, Ceylon and Rodriguez, and soundings in the Indian Ocean in quest of relics of the vanished land.' (*Academy*, June 13, 1874, p. 664.)

NOTE E, page 126.

ON THE COMMON ORIGIN OF FAIRY TALES.

A full discussion of this subject would occupy a goodly-sized volume, and it is not my purpose to add anything to what has been stated in the text, except to remark that it does not necessarily follow that European tales whose leading features resemble Eastern tales existed among the undivided Aryans and migrated with the races, it being certain that many of our folk-tales were invented in the story-loving East *after* the Aryans separated and imported into Europe by pilgrims, students, merchants and warriors, whose several avocations were the means of intimately connecting East and West together.

The following list, which by no means pretends to completeness, of the principal books in our own language bearing upon Indo-European folk-lore, and which are within reach, may be of service to any who desire to pursue the subject of comparative mythology.

Baring-Gould's 'Curious Myths of the Middle Ages,' Rivington, 6s.; Busk's 'Folk-Lore of Rome,' Longmans, 12s.; Campbell's 'Popular Tales of the West Highlands,' Edmonston & Douglas, 32s.; Chambers' 'Book of Days,' Chambers, 21s; Cox's 'Aryan Mythology,' Longmans, 28s.; 'Manual of Mythology,' 3s.; 'Tales of Ancient Greece,' 6s. 6d.; Dasent's 'Popular Tales from the Norse' (out of print); 'Tales from the Fjeld,' Chapman & Hall, 10s. 6d.; Denton's 'Serbian Folk-Lore,' Daldy & Co., 10s. 6d.; Fiske's 'Myths and Myth-Makers,' Trübner, 10s. 6d.; Frere's 'Old Deccan Days,' Murray, 6s; Goddard's 'Wonderful Stories from Northern Lands,' Longmans, 5s.; Gammer Grethel's 'Fairy Tales,' Bohn, 3s. 6d. (and other publishers; these tales being translations of Grimm's *Kinderund Hausmärchen*, or Nursery and Fireside Stories); Gubernati's 'Zoological Mythology,' Trübner, 28s.; Halliwell's 'Popular Nursery Rhymes,' Warne, 3s. 6d.; Hardy's 'Legends and Theories of the Buddhists,' Williams & Norgate, 7s. 6d; 'Játaka,' Páli text and Translation, by Fausböll, Trübner, 16s. 6d.; Johnson's 'Hitopadesa,' Allen & Co., 5s.; Max Müller's 'Hitopadesa,' 2 vols., Longmans, 15s.; Keightley's 'Fairy Mythology,' Bohn, 5s.; Kelly's 'Curiosities of Indo-European Tradition and Folk-Lore,' Chapman & Hall (out of print); Lane's 'Arabian Nights' (out of print; although the tales are from a Semitic people, they are valuable for purposes of comparison); Mallet's 'Northern Antiquities,' Bohn, 5s.; Max Müller's 'Chips from a German Workshop,' 2 vols., Longmans, 24s.; Muir's 'Original Sanskrit Texts,' 5 vols., Trübner; Ralston's 'Songs of the Russian People,' Daldy & Co., 5s.; Ralston's 'Russian Folk-Tales,' Smith, Elder & Co., 12s.; 'Slavonic Fairy Tales,' trans. by Naaké, H. S. King & Co., 5s.; Thorpe's 'Northern Mythology' (out of print); Tylor's 'Early Hist. of Mankind,' Murray, 12s.; Tylor's 'Primitive Culture,' 2 vols. (more particularly volume 1), Murray, 24s.; Brand's 'Popular Antiquities,' 3 vols., Bohn, 15s.; Murray's 'Manual of Mythology,' Asher & Co., 9s.

NOTE F, page 138.

THE SACRED BOOKS OF HINDUISM.

The sacred literature of Hinduism comprises the four *Vedas* and certain mystical and philosophical books connected with them, as the *Âranyakas* and *Upanishads*; the *Sûtras* or brief digest of sacrificial rules and Brahmanic meditations; the *Purânas* and *Tantras*, upon which the popular creed is founded; while closely related to the earlier period of Hinduism are two epic poems not inaptly spoken of as the Iliad and Odyssey of the East, and entitled the *Râmâyana* and *Mahâbhârata*. There is also a celebrated law-book, known as the *Institutes of Menu* or *Manu*, from which the Hindu legend of the creation given at p. 24 is quoted, and which treats of religious as well as legal subjects.

Under the general name of Vedas there are included four collections of hymns, of which the Rig-Veda is the oldest and most important, the others consisting mainly of extracts from it. The collections are respectively known as the

Rig-Veda,	Veda of Hymns of Praise.
Sâma-Veda,	Veda of Chants.
Yagur-Veda,	Veda of Sacrificial Formulas.
Atharva-Veda (also called Brahma-Veda),	Veda of Incantations.

Each Veda consists of two portions; Sanhitâ or *collection* of Mantras or *hymns*, and Brâhmana, which gives 'information on the proper use of the hymns at sacrifices, on their sacred meaning, on their supposed authors, and similar topics.' On the authorship and final collection of the Vedic hymns Dr Muir remarks : 'For many ages the successive generations of these ancient rishis continued to make new contributions to the stock of hymns, while they carefully preserved those which had been handed down to them by their forefathers. The fact of this successive composition of the hymns is evident from the ancient index to the Rig-Veda, which shows that these compositions are ascribed to different generations of the same family as their " seers." The descendants of the most celebrated rishis would no doubt form complete collections of the hymns which had been composed by their respective ancestors. After being thus handed down, with little alteration, in the families of the original authors for several centuries, during which many of them were continually applied to the purposes of religious worship, these hymns, which had been gathering an accumulated sanctity throughout all this period, were at length collected in one great body of sacred literature, styled the Sanhitâ of the Rig-Veda—a work which in the Purânas is assigned to Vedavyâsa and one of his pupils.' (Origl. Sanskrit Texts, Part II. pp. 206, *et seq.*)

Of the ten books which compose the Rig-Veda, the first book contains 191 hymns. The hymns to Agni are placed first, then those to Indra, followed by those addressed to other leading deities. The contents of the next six books are arranged in like manner and are each ascribed to a single poet or poetic family; 'thus far we seem to have a single collection made and ordered by the same hand.' Of the remaining books, the ninth is notable because the whole of its hymns, 114 in number, are addressed to the Soma, while the tenth book, the contents of which are of various authorship, has the same number of hymns as the first book.

The Sâma-Veda consists entirely of verses from the Rig-Veda which were chanted at the Soma-ritual. The verses composing the Sanhitâ of the Yagur-Veda were chiefly selected from the Rig-Veda for muttering during various sacrificial ceremonies. The fourth Veda contains, in addition to selections from the Rig-Veda, hymns of a later age addressed to gods who are objects of fear to their cringing worshippers, and to a multitude of demons whom the suppliants seek to appease by promises and bribes.

Of the Brâhmanas attached to each Veda, attention can here be called only to the Satapatha-Brâhmana which is appended to the White or later portion of the Yagur-Veda and which in addition to descriptions of various festivals, has some curious stories, one of which narrates the Deluge (See Max Müller's Anct. Sans. Literature, p. 425). The relation of the Brâhmanas to the metrical portion of the Vedas may be compared to that of the writings of the Fathers to the New Testament or to that of the Talmud to the Old Testament, but, as already stated in the text, they are regarded, like the hymns, as divinely inspired.

The opinions of Sanskrit scholars differ as to the age of the oldest hymns of the Rig-Veda, Dr Haug placing them as far back as B.C. 2400; Prof. Whitney between B.C. 1600 and B.C. 2000; and Prof. Max Müller B.C. 1200 to B.C. 1500. (For discussion upon the probable date of the oldest portion of the Rig-Veda, see Whitney's 'Oriental and Linguistic Studies,' pp. 21, 73, and Max Müller's 'Chips,' vol. i., pp. 11, 114). The Sûtras (meaning 'string' or 'thread') consist of strings of short sentences explaining and giving directions concerning public and household religious rites and stating in pithy form the long result of Brâhmanic thought and speculation. They are greatly revered and out of those portions which deal with public and private duties the famous Laws or Institutes of Manu have been developed. There are also six works, known as the Vedângas, or 'limbs of the Veda,' which treat of the grammar, metre, proper pronunciation (a matter of as much importance in Brahmanic eyes as correct understanding) of the Vedic texts. The chief object of one Vedânga is 'to convey such knowledge of the heavenly bodies as is necessary for fixing correctly the days and hours of the Vedic sacrifices.'

The Âranyakas (from *âranya*, a forest) are treatises which were 'prepared for the edification of those who have retired to live a life of contemplative solitude and asceticism in the woods, as it is theoretically the duty of every Brahmanic householder to do, after a certain period of life,' and the Upanishads are works closely related to the above, but giving amplitude to meditations on the questions which have ever perplexed the human mind and which called forth vain reply in those great systems of Hindu philosophy which arose many centuries before Christ.

From this outline, naked and incomplete as it is, we may yet see what a vast body of literature the Rig-Veda-Sanhitâ gathered round itself, a literature the age of which may never be accurately known, but the antiquity of which is beyond question.

The Râmâyana and Mahâbhârata, both of which, certain portions excepted, were doubtless written before the rise of Buddhism, form, together with the Purânas, the popular sacred literature of the Hindus, the great mass of whom are wholly ignorant of the Veda and its connected writings. The Râmâyana is the work of one author and mainly narrates the history of Râma, the seventh incarnation or avatar of Vishnu, whose supremacy is upheld throughout the poem. Amidst much that is absurd there are passages of exceeding tenderness and grace, as the following episode shows. Râma's father had in a moment of weakness promised to grant one of his queens any two boons she might please to ask, and she, jealous that Râma might supplant her own son in the throne, requested his banishment. When he is gone, the remorse of the king is great, and there rises before him the memory of a death which he had accidentally caused when a young man. He tells his favourite queen how, when hunting, his arrow by mischance shot a poor boy who was the comfort of his parents, and how as the father leaned over the body he besought the still tongue to speak :

'Come, dear child, embrace thy father; put thy little hand in mine ;
Let me hear thee sweetly prattle some fond, playful word of thine.
Ah ! who 'll read me now the Vedas, filling my own heart with joy ?
Who, when evening rites are over, cheer me, mourning for my boy ?
Who will bring me fruits and water, roots and wild herbs from the wood ?
Who supply the helpless hermit, like a cherish'd guest, with food ?
Can I tend thine aged mother till her weary life is done ?
Can I feed her, soothe her sorrow,—longing for her darling son ?'

The king then tells how the father cursed him for the deed and said, ' For this thing that thou hast done, as I mourn for my beloved, thou shalt sorrow for a son,' and he feels that the day of the prophecy's sad fulfilment has come. Such pathetic incidents as this and, to borrow a more familiar example, the touching tribute to a mother's tenderness in the hour of need which is told in 2 Kings iv. 18-20, move us more than the story of kingcraft in which each is imbedded.

The Mahâbhârata, or ' great history of the descendants of Bhârata,' contains above 200,000 lines, and is the work of different authors at different periods. It is a story of quarrels between rival families, whose adventures and wars do not however occupy more than one-fourth of the narrative, the remaining three-fourths consisting of a variety of episodes and legends, amongst which latter is one of the Deluge closely resembling that given in the Satapatha-Brâhmana, but told at greater length ; one incident being that when the flood was over it was discovered that among the treasures which had been lost was the 'Amrita, or Drink of Immortality.' The gods met in council to consider how the loss might be repaired, when Vishnu advises them to churn the ocean that the vexed sea might give back its spoil. With the aid of Brahmâ and the King of the Serpents the lost Amrita is recovered. We see from this incident that the Vedic gods had fallen from their high places, and were no longer regarded as immortal, except through partaking of the beverage of immortality. The Mahâbhârata is noted for a deeply religious and philosophical poem called the 'Bhagavad-Gîtâ, *i.e.*, 'Revelations from the Deity,' which is interwoven in the midst of a battle scene.

The Purânas, which are barely a thousand years old, are eighteen in number. Their contents are very miscellaneous, embracing cosmogony, legends (many of which are derived from the Mahâbhârata and cast in an expanded form), genealogies of the gods, directions about festivals, &c., all written in the form of dialogue and presented in a style which secures their being widely read by the common people. They are evidently of priestly origin, one main object in their compilation being the exaltation of Vishnu and Siva, each of whom has Purânas written to his praise and glory; Vishnu more than Siva. The Tantras are certain works in which directions are given for the correct performance of rites in honour of the 'energy' or wife of Siva, many of which are of a debasing kind.

The sacred literature of Hinduism thus shows three distinct periods in the history of that religion: 1st, the Vedic, represented by the Vedas (the fourth Veda excepted, as being the latest), Sûtras and forest-treatises; 2d, the Brahmanic, by the laws of Manu and the Epic poems, a period during which the systems of philosophy, the Hindu triad, the division of people into caste, &c., arose; and, Buddhism having in the meantime risen and declined, 3d, the modern Hindu, represented by the Purânas and kindred works.

Very much of interest, which is beyond the province of this book to deal with, awaits the student of the secular literature of India,—its dramas, fictions, lyric poetry and fables. Of these a very able analysis is given in Manning's 'Ancient and Mediæval India' (Allen & Co., 30s.); while all that the ordinary reader would care to know concerning the Vedic and Brahmanic periods and the contents of the two great epics and leading dramas is given in a condensed but lively form in Talboys Wheeler's 'Hist. of India' (Trübner & Co., 3 vols., 57s.), Miss Richardson's 'Iliad of the East' (Macmillan & Co., 7s. 6d), and Mr Griffiths' 'Specimens of Indian Poetry' (Trübner & Co., 6s.); Mr Griffiths has also recently completed a translation of the 'Râmâyana' (Trübner & Co., 84s.); while the Mahâbhârata is the subject of a learned article in the *Westminster Review*, April 1868. For full information on the matters of this Note the most valuable and accessible books are Prof. H. H. Wilson's Works (especially vols. vi.-x. for the contents of the Purânas); Colebrooke's Essays; Muir's Sanskrit Texts; Max Müller's Rig-Veda; all which are published by Messrs Trübner & Co., but, owing unfortunately to the limited number of readers among whom they circulate, somewhat high-priced.

NOTE G, page 150.

ON THE WORDS BRAHMĂ OR BRAHM AND BRAHMÂ.

Brahmă or Brahm is the nominative singular of the neuter noun Bráhman, which meant originally 'force, will, wish, and the propulsive power of creation.' 'But,' remarks Professor Max Müller, 'this impersonal bráhman as soon as it is named grows into something strange and divine. It ends by being one of many gods, one of the great triad worshipped to the present day.' Brahmâ is the nominative singular of the masculine noun.

NOTE H, page 159.

THE SACRED BOOKS OF THE PÂRSÎ RELIGION.

By the name Zend-Avesta, or, as the native scholars have it, Avesta-Zend, 'text or scripture' and 'commentary,' is said to be signified, but the meaning of the words is uncertain. The books included under this title are ascribed by the Pârsîs to Zoroaster, to whom it was said God revealed them in the form of conversations, as, according to the Old Testament, He talked with Moses. But with the exception of the Gâthâs, which are the oldest portion, and which may embody what Zoroaster communicated to his disciples, the Avesta is probably, as its fragmentary character denotes, the result of tradition gathered from many sources.

It consists of the *Yazna*, the *Vispered*, which together with a third portion, the *Vendidâd*, make up the *Vendidâd Sâde;* and the *Yesht*, which added to some smaller pieces, composes the *Khordeh-Avesta*, or 'lesser Avesta.'

These include the *Avesta* proper, which is written in an ancient Persian language, from which the modern dialects of Persia are probably descended. Attached to the Avesta are translations and explanations of its text, some written in Pehlevî, an ancient mixed language, and others in Pârsî, an older form of the modern Persian. To this additional matter the name *Zend* is more correctly given; and besides this, there are still later additions, the most prominent of which is the *Bundehesh*, a digest of Zoroastrian scriptures and doctrines. The principal portion of the Avesta is the Yazna (from a word allied to the Sanskrit *yajna*, meaning 'sacrifice'). It consists of seventy-two chapters, many of which drily detail the chief 'personages and objects recognized by the Zoroastrian religion, while the remaining and older portion is of greater interest. It includes the Gâthâs, five collections of unrhymed metrical hymns, which, speaking broadly, are related to the rest as the Rig-veda to the Brâhmanas. The first hymn is headed 'The Revealed Thought, the Revealed Word, the Revealed Deed of Zarathustra the Holy; the Archangel's first song, the Gâthâs.' 'They are all more or less devoted to exhortations on the part of the prophet to forsake the *devas* (see p. 160), and to bow only before Ahuramazdâ,' to whom, as well as to his angels, and to earth, fire, water, &c., prayers are addressed in other portions of the Yazna and also the Vispered. The Vendidâd embodies the moral and ceremonial code, by which a man may keep pure. The whole is in the form of conversations beween Ormuzd and Zoroaster, and the first part recites the sixteen Aryan countries referred to at p. 70; the second part treats of laws and ceremonies; the third part of spells against evil spirits and diseases. The Yesht contains the germ of legends introduced into the great Persian epic, the Shahnameh, and addresses to the archangels, the sun, the heavenly fountain, the souls of the departed, &c.

I hope that enough has been said in the brief chapter on Zoroastrianism to show that it is not easy to over-estimate the importance of the Avesta as a guide to our knowledge of a religion, noblest and purest of the ancient faiths, and the influence of which upon surrounding and subsequent beliefs was marked. (Spiegel's 'Avesta, die heiligen schriften der parsen,' tr. Bleek; Dr Haug's Essays, a reprint of which is much to be desired; Whitney's 'Oriental, &c., Studies,' art. 'Avesta;' and Müller's 'Chips,' vol. i., are among the leading authorities. On the use of the word 'Zend,' see Max Müller's 'Lect. on Language,' vol. i. p. 237, 6th edit.)

NOTE I, page 171.

LEGENDS RELATING TO THE BIRTH OF BUDDHA.

The belief in transmigration is common to both Brahmanism and Buddhism, and abundant illustration of this is afforded in the histories of the five hundred and fifty former births of Buddha narrated in the Játaka, to which reference was made at page 124. In the legend concerning him which Bishop Bigandet has translated from the Burmese (itself apparently a compilation from a MS. in the Pali, or sacred language of the Buddhist literature), it is said, that while dwelling in the abode of the Nats, living a life of contemplation, he received the news that, having passed through the needful preceding stages of existence, he was to become a Buddha, the twenty-fifth of that name who have appeared in the world to open for men the way to deliverance. According to the Buddhists, the places of different orders of beings are arranged as follows, extending from the bottom of the earth to a measureless height above it. Lowest of all are the four states of punishment; then the abode of man; above this the six seats of Nats, beings who play a great part in the affairs of the world, and who are akin to the spirits a belief in whom is common to all religions; above these dwell the Brahmas, who are free from all low passions, yet not fully weaned from love of the world. Above these are seats occupied by the Arupa, who have reached the summit of perfection, and whom one step farther will carry into Nirvana. After a while, the future Buddha, then known as Phralaong, having received the congratulations of the Nats, and made choice of birth in a princely caste as befitting his high calling, descended to earth, and at that moment great wonders appeared ; a radiant light was spread over ten thousand worlds; the blind saw, the dumb spake, the lame walked, the deformed stood erect, prisoners were freed ; refreshing breezes blew gently over the earth ; cooling springs burst forth, and soft showers fell ; flowers of richest colour bloomed; lilies dropped from the sky, scattering sweet scent around ; the songs of the Nats were heard by the glad ears of men, and the choicest perfumes were diffused through the air. Then came from their high abode spirits to watch over the palace where the child was to be born, and to ward off harm from him and his royal mother, whose soul rested in a perfect calm. Then in due time the child was born, and at once stood erect before the wondering men and spirits, while, leaping, he said, ' This is my last birth; there shall be to me no other state of existence ; I am the greatest of all beings.' At his birth there sprang from out the ground the famous tree, under the shadow of which he was to become Buddha. 'The Bo-tree is the "pippul" (*Ficus religiosa*) of India. It differs from the Banyan (*F. Indica*) by sending down no roots from its branches. Its heart-shaped leaves, with long attenuated points, are attached to the stem by so slender a stalk that they appear in the profoundest calm to be ever in motion; and thus, like the leaves of the aspen, which, from the tradition that the cross was made of that wood, the Syrians believe to tremble in recollection of the events of the crucifixion of Christ, those of the Bo-tree are supposed by Buddhists to exhibit a tremulous veneration associated with the sacred scenes of which they were the witnesses.' ('Tennent's Ceylon,' Vol. I., p. 342.) Among the people who came, glad-hearted, at the news of the wonderful child's birth, special mention is made in the legends of a devout old man, reminding us of Simeon, who, for his great holiness, had the gift of prophecy. Although joy overflowed his soul at the great future which lay before the child, his eyes filled with tears because he knew that he should not live to see it. Seven days after the birth of Theidat, for so they named the child, because of the service he was to render to mankind, his mother died, and for her virtues was taken to the dwelling-place of the Nats.

Bishop Bigandet remarks ('Legend,' &c., p. 16), that 'it must be confessed that the conception of Phralaong in his mother's womb is wrapped up in a mysterious obscurity which appears to exclude the idea of conjugal intercourse. The Cochin-Chinese in their religious legends, pretend that Buddha was conceived and born from Maia in a wonderful manner, not resembling at all what takes place according to the law of nature.' In giving 543 B.C. as the date of Buddha's death, I have followed that generally received as based on the Sinhalese authorities. Some, however, place that event a century or more later, which, in so uncertain a matter as the older Hindu chronology, is not a very remarkable difference.

NOTE K, page 177.

THE SACRED BOOKS OF BUDDHISM.

The Tripitaka or sacred canon of the Buddhists is in three divisions, the Vinaya-pitaka; the Sutta-pitaka; and the Abhidhamma-pitaka; the second and third pitakas being 'sometimes comprehended under the general name of Dharma or law.' Pali, the sacred language of the Buddhists, is an ancient dialect, related to the Vedic Sanskrit as Italian is related to Latin, and was once spoken in that part of India where Buddhism had its rise. In their belief that it is divine and the parent of all other languages, the Buddhists form no exception to some other religionists in their notion concerning the language of their sacred books. (See Max Müller's 'Lect. on Language,' vol. i. pp. 146, 161, 6th edit.) The Tripitaka, which was found to exist in Sanskrit also, has been translated into the languages of the different countries where Buddhism was propagated; into Tibetan, Mongolian, Chinese, Burmese, &c., but for our most accurate knowledge respecting it we are largely indebted to the materials furnished by the island of Ceylon, among which are two works of great value, the Dipavansa, or history of Buddhism in Ceylon, and the Mahavansa, a history of that island from the earliest times to the fourth century after Christ.

The canonical books and their commentaries form a mass of literature bewildering in its vastness; the three Pitakas alone extending to 592,000 stanzas, and the Atthakathá or commentaries, containing 361,550 more. According to a statement quoted by Spence Hardy in his 'Legends and Theories of the Buddhists,' the canon contains 29,368,000 letters, (five or six times more than the Bible contains,) and Max Müller tells us that 'the Tibetan edition of the Buddhist canon, consisting of two collections, the Kanjur and the Tanjur, numbers about 325 volumes folio, each weighing in the Pekin edition from four to five pounds. The Sutta-pitaka, which contains the discourses of Buddha, comprises five separate works, the last of which is composed of fifteen books, the second being the 'Dhammapada,' or 'path of virtue' (see p. 181). The most popular portion of this pitaka are the sûtras or discourses concerning his 550 births, which profess to have been narrated by Buddha himself, and which are embraced under the title 'Pansiya-panas-játakapota.' Messrs Trübner make the welcome announcement of an edition of the 'Játaka,' comprising Pali text edited by Faüsboll and English translation by Childers. Upon Buddhism generally, see Rev. Spence Hardy's 'Manual' (out of print); 'Eastern Monachism' and 'Legends and Theories of the Buddhists' (Williams & Norgate, 7s. 6d. each); Bigandet's 'Legend of Gaudama,' from the Burmese (Trübner & Co., 18s.); 'Buddhagosha's Parables,' prefaced by Max Müller's translation of the 'Dhammapada' (Trübner & Co., 12s. 6d.); Sir M. C. Swámy's 'Sutta Nipáta,' a translation of certain discourses from the Sutta-pitaka (Trübner, 6s.); Alabaster's 'Wheel of the Law' (Trübner, 14s); Max Müller's 'Chips,' vol. i.; also his 'Introduction to the Science of Religion' (Longmans, 10s. 6d.); Bartélemy Saint-Hilaire's 'Le Bouddha et sa Religion' (Paris, 1860); Eugene Burnouf's 'Introduction à l'Histoire du Buddhisme indien' (Paris, 1844); Schlagintweit's 'Buddhism in Tibet' (Trübner & Co., 42s.); Otto Kistner's 'Buddha and his Doctrines' (Trübner, 2s. 6d); Beal's 'Travels of Fah-Hian and Sung-Yun' (Trübner, 10s. 6d.); Ib. 'Catena of Buddhist Scriptures' (Trübner, 15s.); Cunningham's 'Bhilsa Topes,' or Buddhist Monuments of Central India (Trübner, 21s.); the Journals of the Royal Asiatic Society, the works of Bunsen, Colebrooke, Ferguson Wilson, &c.

NOTE L, page 195.

THE SACRED BOOKS, OR CLASSICS, OF THE CHINESE.

In giving an account of the books included under this name, Dr Legge tells us that those now recognized as of highest authority in China are comprehended under the denominations of 'The Five King' and 'The Four Shoo.'

'The Five King' are the five canonical works, containing the truths upon the highest subjects from the sages of China, and which should be received as law by all generations. The term *shoo* simply means 'writings' or 'books.' ('The Chinese Classics,' vol. i., p. 1.) The Five King are the *Yih,* or 'Book of Changes;' the *Shoo,* or 'Book of Historical Documents;' the *She,* or 'Book of Poetry;' the *Le-Ke,* or 'Record of Rites;' and the *Ch'un Ts'ew* or 'Spring and Autumn,' annals extending from B.C. 721 to 480.

Confucius made some additions to the Yih, Shoo and She, but 'the Ch'un Ts'ew is the only one of the Five King which can, with an approximation to correctness, be described as of his own " making." '

The four books are the *Lun Yu,* occupied chiefly with the sayings of Confucius; the *Ta Hëŏ,* or 'Great Learning,' by Tsang-Sin, a disciple of Confucius; the *Chung Yung* or 'Doctrine of the Mean' (these three works will be found fully analysed in the first vol. of Legge's 'Chinese Classics') and the *Works of Mencius,* the 'Master's' most illustrious disciple. 'After the death of Confucius, there was an end of his exquisite words; and when his seventy disciples had passed away, violence began to be done to their meaning.' So runs the ancient chronicle, from which we further learn that to keep the people in ignorance the courtiers persuaded the Emperors of the Ts'in dynasty (B.C. 220-205) to burn the sacred books and the writings of the philosophers, and to slaughter a large number of scholars for keeping copies of the forbidden books. But when the Emperors of the Han dynasty came to the throne they set themselves to repair the loss, and by great effort succeeded in recovering the ancient literature, since which 'the successive dynasties have considered the literary monuments of the country to be an object of their special care,' and Dr Legge is satisfied that the evidence is complete that the classical books of China have come down from at least a century before the Christian era, substantially the same as we have them at present.

See Legge's 'Life and Teachings of Confucius,' 10s. 6d.; Ib. 'Works of Mencius,' 12s.; Ib. 'Chinese Classics,' £16, 16s, (Trübner); Freeman Clarke's 'Ten Great Religions' (Trübner, 14s.); and the works of Archdeacon Hardwick, Doolittle, Meadows, &c.

The mere recital of the names of the sacred books which has filled the larger portion of these Notes indicates how impossible it is within the limits of a single life to acquire full knowledge of the book-religions of the world alone. And when we remember how hard it is to understand the nature of the doctrinal differences which divide Christendom into many sects, and to master the meaning of the technical terms of the separate organizations, we must not wonder if we fail to discern clearly the salient features of religions in the study of which these difficulties are multiplied a thousand-fold. But one thing we surely cannot fail to learn: the lesson of a larger charity towards all.

INDEX.

A.

'Abou Ben Adhem,' legend of, 253.
Abraham and Ishmael, Muslim legend of, 211.
" and Zoroaster, 159.
Adam, Muslim legend about, 211.
" and Eve, 47.
Africa, spread of Islám in, 224.
Age, probable, of deposits in 'Kent's Hole,' 59.
" " of Vedic hymns, 266.
Agni, god of fire, 139, 148, 150, 265.
" birth of, and Vedic hymn to, 140.
Ahaná and Athênê, 101.
Ahriman, Persian god of darkness, 23, 46, 70, 161, 164, 168.
Ahura Mazdâ, *see* Ormuzd.
Airyanem-Vaêgô, the Persian Eden, 70.
Al-Ilâh, Allâh, 202.
All-Father (Alfadir), 7, 27, 215.
Altar, 91, 92.
" of Agni, 148.
" offerings by Aryans upon, 94.
Ancestors, offerings to spirits of, 148.
" worship of, 190.
Angels, Buddhist belief in, 273.
" Mohammadan " 214.
" Zoroastrian " 160.
'Angra-Mainyus' (Ahriman), 161.
Animals, criminality of, 50, 259.
Antiquity of man in Europe, 56, 59, 61.
Apollo and Pythôn, myth of, 106.
Arabs, character of the, 210.
" figurative language of, 236.
" past influence of, in Europe, 225.
Aranyakas, 264, 267.
'Arya,' meaning of, 68.
Aryan civilization, 75.
" languages, table of, 83.
" myths and fairy tales, 96-128.
" religion, 86-96.
" tribes, 67.

Aryan tribes, separation of, 128.
Aryans, division among the Eastern, 133.
" source of knowledge about, 79.
Asgard, abode of the Norse gods, 27.
Asoka, king, 182.
Ass in the lion's skin, 125.
Assyrian legend of the Creation, etc., 255.
Atharva-Veda, 264, 266.
Athênê, myth of, 101.
Atlantis, lost island of, 37.
Atthakathá, 276.
Attraction, law of, 31, 33.
Avatárs of Vishnu, 153, 267.
Avesta-Zend, *see* Zend-Avesta.

B.

Baal, a Semitic god, 202.
Bab-il, 201.
Babylon, captivity of Jews in, 166, 167.
Babylonian legend of the Creation, 22, 255.
" " Flood, 72.
" " Tower of Babel, 73.
Bactria, 75, 85, 158, 163.
Baker, Sir Samuel, quoted, 236.
Beast-fables, 125.
'Beauty and the Beast,' variants of, 5, 120-124.
Bel, a Semitic god, 202.
Belus, " 23.
Berosus, 22.
Beth-el, 201.
Bhagavad-Gitâ, 269.
Bible, mode of study of the, 230.
" origin and growth of, 232, 238.
" inspiration of, 235.
Birth of Buddha, legends relating to the, 273.
Birthplace of mankind, supposed, 38, 53, 260.

INDEX.

Black Stone, the, 208, 211, 214.
Books, sacred, *see* Sacred Books.
Bo-Tree, 274.
Brahmā, 24, 150, 270.
  ,, creation of heaven and earth by, 25.
Brahmâ, 151, etc., 269, 270.
Brahma-Veda, 264, 266.
Brahman, Buddha and the, 179.
Brâhmanas, 139, 264, 266.
Brahmans, rise of the, 151.
  ,, tyranny of the, 151.
Brahmanism, *see* Hinduism.
Bridge of souls, 164, 223.
Britain, Great, more than once beneath the sea, 37, 55.
'Brother,' meaning of, 77.
Brutes, difference between man and, 49, 54.
  ,, punished as criminals, 50, 259.
Buddha, life of, sketch of the, 171-176.
  ,, as ninth descent of Vishnu, 154.
  ,, leading doctrines taught by, 183.
  ,, legends as to the birth of, 273.
  ,, stories concerning, 178.
  ,, teaching of, 180-182.
Buddha's death, date of, 275.
  ,, four paths to Nirvâna, 184.
  ,, ten commandments, 185.
Buddhism, countries professing, 182.
  ,, and Roman Catholicism, likeness between, 187.
  ,, a state religion of China, 191.
  ,, rise and decay of, in India, 182.
  ,, source of success of, 185.
Buddhist councils, 176.
  ,, fables, *see* Játaka.
  ,, forms of worship, 187.
  ,, legends of the past, 44.
  ,, scriptures, 177.
Bull and cows, mythical, 108.
  ,, worship of, 155.
Burning of body, 148.
  ,, of remains of Buddha, 176.

C.

Caste, 151, 185.
Caverns, discovery of stone implements in, 56.
Celtic languages, 84.
Celtic races, 67, 85.
  ,, migration to Europe, 130.
Ceylon, Buddhist relics and literature in, 183, 275.
Chaldean and Jewish legends, relation between, 255.
  ,, legend of the Flood, 72.
  ,, ,, Tower of Babel, 73.
Chalk, nature and rate of deposit of, 39.
Changes on the earth's surface, 4, 37, 55.
Charity, Mohammad's sermon on, 216.
Child-life as illustrative of myth-making, 103.
China, religions of, 189, etc.
  ,, sacred books of, 195, 277.
Chinese language, 82.
  ,, manners and customs, 189.
  ,, reverence for learning, 190.
  ,, worship of ancestors, 190.
Christ, Muslim reverence for, 213.
Christian religion, relation of, to other religions, 246.
Christians in Arabia, 212.
Cinderella, origin and variants of tale of, 5, 117-120.
Civilization of the Aryans, 75.
  ,, of pre-Aryan races, 65, 134.
Climate of Europe, changes in, 54, 55.
Comets, origin of, 31.
Commandments, ten, of Buddha, 185.
Confucius, sketch of the life of, 192-194.
  ,, teaching of, 196, 197.
Cooling of sun, planets, and moons, 34.
Councils, Buddhist, 176.
Creation, legends of, in Genesis, 13-15.
  ,, Babylonian legend of, 22, 255.
  ,, Egyptian, 23.
  ,, Greek, 27.
  ,, Hindu, 24.
  ,, Persian, 23.
  ,, Scandinavian, 25.
  ,, of man, 23, 26, 28, 48, 50, 52.
  ,, told by Science, 29, etc.
Criminality of animals, etc., 50, 259.
Crust of the earth, 33, 36, 39, 40.
Cyrus, 166, 259.

D.

'Daughter,' meaning of, 77.
Dawn as a source of myth, 104.

INDEX.

'Day,' meaning of, in Genesis, 20.
Dead body dreaded by the Pârsîs, 167.
Death, Buddha on the law of, 179.
  ,, Confucius on, 195.
  ,, of Mohammad, 221.
  ,, Norsemen's idea of, 27.
  ,, date of Buddha's, 275.
'Deity,' origin of word, 88.
Deluge, see Flood.
Deodand, 260.
Deus, same as Dyaus, Zeus, etc., 88.
Deva (blight), 88.
Devas (bad spirits), 70, 160.
Development of man's higher nature, 249.
Devil, the, 48, 106, 168, 256.
  ,, temptation of Buddha by, 174.
Dhammapada, 181, 276.
'Div,' a form of dyu, 88.
Dyaus, chief Aryan god, 88.
  ,, displaced by Indra, 141.
  ,, same as Zeus, etc., 88.
  ,, -pítar, same as Jupiter, 89.

E.

'Earth,' meaning of, 68.
  ,, changes in surface of the, 4, 37, 55.
  ,, crust of the, 33, 36, 39.
  ,, future of the, 35.
  ,, invoked as 'mother,' 87, 139, 149.
  ,, once a sun, 34.
  ,, store of heat in the, 34.
Eastern Aryans, 132, 148.
'Eddas,' meaning of, 26, 27.
Eden, Garden of, 15, 42, 257.
  ,, ,, Persian, 70.
Egg, notion that heaven and earth are made from an, 25.
Egypt, religion of ancient, 241.
Egyptian legend of the Creation, 23.
Eight steps to Nirvâna, Buddha's, 185.
El, a Semitic god, 201.
Elves, 97.
Epic poems of Aryan nations as outgrowth of myth, 98.
'Erin,' probably allied to 'Aryan,' 69.
Erinyes, the Greek Furies, 112.
Eskimos, 61.
Europe, changes in climate and surface of, 54, 55, 56.
  ,, antiquity of man in, 56, 59, 61.
  ,, early races in, 61-63.

Europe, migration of Aryans to, 130.
Evil, source of, 169.

F.

Fairy Tales, common origin of many, 98, etc.
  ,, Beauty and the Beast, 120-124.
  ,, Cinderella, 117-120.
  ,, Giant who had no heart in his body, 121.
  ,, House that Jack Built, 126
  ,, Jinn's soul, 123.
  ,, Punchkin, 122.
Family life, Aryan, 77.
'Father,' meaning of, 77.
Finns, language of the, 83.
  ,, notion of, about heaven and earth, 25.
Fire, worship of, 139, 164.
  ,, -god, Agni, 140.
  ,, ,, hymn to, 141.
Flood, legends of a, 71, 72, 74, 257, 268.
Fo, the Chinese name of Buddha, 191.
Forces of nature, 31.
Four paths to Nirvâna, Buddha's, 184.
Freyja, the 'lady,' 215.
Frog, the sun as a, 112.
Frost-giants, 26.
Funeral hymn, Hindu, 149.
Future life, belief in a, 147, 164, 166, 186, 211, 223, 242, 243.

G.

Ganges, River, 155.
Garden of Eden, 15, 42, 70, 257.
Gâthâs, 161, 271, 272.
Gautama Buddha, 171.
Gellert, myth of the hound, 98, 115.
Genesis, legends of creation in, 13-15.
  ,, creation of man in, 48-50.
  ,, meaning of 'day' in, 20.
Giant who had no heart in his body, 121
Glacial Epoch, see Ice Age.
Gloaming, Nurse, 105.
'Goddess of Speech,' 95.
Gods, Aryan, 89.
  ,, Semitic, 201, 202.
  ,, Vedic, 139.
Grand Lama, the, 188.
Greece, religion of ancient, 242.
Greek language, 84.
  ,, legend of the creation, 27.

INDEX.

Greek legend of the first man, 45.
," myths, meaning of the, 100-102, 110-112.
'Grimm's law,' 81.
Gypsies, language of the, 83.

H.

Heat, nature of, 32.
," store of, inside the earth, 34.
Heaven and Earth, creation of, by Brahma, 25.
," ," as father and mother, 89.
Hebrew language, source of, 202.
Hel, Hela, goddess, 215, 244.
Hercules and Cacus, myth of, 106.
Hesiod, 27.
Hindu legend of the Creation, 24.
," ," Deluge, 266, 268.
," funeral hymn, 149.
," Trinity, 139, 152.
Hinduism, ancient and modern, 136, etc.
," present condition of, 155.
Hindus, ancient prayer of the, 143.
," ," belief of, in a future life, 147.
Hira, Mount, 209, 226.
Homa-offering, 164.
Horse, sacrifice of the, 95.
House that Jack built, 126.
Hungarian language, 83.
Huxley, Professor, quoted, 37.

I.

Ice Age, 55, 61.
Il, Ilu, a Semitic god, 72, 201.
Ilâh, 202.
Inanimate things, criminality of, 259.
Incarnation of Buddha, 274, 275.
," Vishnu, 153, 154, 267.
India, races in, 134.
Indo-European, see Aryan.
Indra, myth of, 106, 109.
," Vedic god of the sky, 139, 141, 150, 160, 265.
," birth of, 141.
," hymn to, 142.
Inscriptions in 'Kent's Hole,' 58.
Inspiration of the Bible, etc., 231.
," defined, 240.
," **theories of, 235**

Institutes of Manu, 24, 78, 264, 266
Ishmael, Arab legend of, 215.
'Islám,' meaning of, 204.
Islám, doctrines of, 213, 217, 223.
," spread of, 221, 223, 224.
," wars of, 222, 225.

J.

Jah, Jahveh (Jehovah), 202.
Jainas, Hindu sect of, 156.
Játaka (Buddhist fables), 124, 273, 276.
Jewish history, importance of, 203.
," legends of the creation, 13-15.
," ," of man, 48-50.
," ," Adam and Eve, 47.
," ," relation of, to other legends, 18, 168, 255,
," Sabbath, origin of, 20.
," religion, influence of, on Islám, 214.
Jews, captivity of, in Babylon, 166.
," Mohammad's overtures to the, 221.
," settlement of, in Arabia, 211.
Jovis, same as Dyaus, etc., 88.
Judgment, day of, 164, 223, 242.
Juggernaut, 155.
Jupiter, 89.

K.

Kaabah, sacred stone of the, 208, 211, 214.
Kali, Hindu goddess, 154.
Kansa, Hindu demon-king, 154.
Kapilavastu, 171.
'Kent's Hole,' deposits in, 57.
," ," probable age of, 59, 60.
," inscriptions in, 58.
Kiblah, 220.
'Kings,' sacred books of the Chinese, 195, 278.
Kingsley, Charles, quoted, 129.
Korân, contents of the, 225. 226.
," quotations from the, 216, 218 227-229.
Koreish, Arab tribe of the, 208.
Krishna, Vishnu's avatár as, 153.
," worship of, 155.
Kronos, myth of, 100, 110.
K'ung-Foo-Tse, see Confucius, 192.

INDEX.

L.

Language, value of, as a clue to race, 79-82, 132.
  ,, stages in growth of, 82.
Languages, Aryan, 83.
  ,, ,, words common to, 85.
  ,, Semitic, 200.
Lao-tse, 191.
Laplace, 258.
Latin language, 84.
Law of attraction, 31, 33.
  ,, Grimm's, 81.
Laws of Manu, 24, 78, 264, 266.
Legend of Creation, Babylonian, 22, 255
  ,, ,, Egyptian, 23.
  ,, ,, Greek, 27.
  ,, ,, Hindu, 24.
  ,, ,, Jewish, 13-15.
  ,, ,, Persian, 23.
  ,, ,, Scandinavian, 25.
Legends of birth of Buddha, 273.
  ,, creation of man, 48-50, etc.
  ,, Flood, 71, 72, 268.
  ,, Man's happy state, 44-47, 71.
  ,, Mohammad, 205.
  ,, Tower of Babel, 73.
  ,, relation between Jewish and Chaldean, 255.
Light and darkness, myths of, 109.
Limestone caverns, 56.

M.

Magic hatchets, scissors, etc., 124.
Mahâbhârata, 264, 268.
'Man,' meaning of, 49.
Man, antiquity of, in Europe, 56, 59-61.
  ,, difference between, and brute, 49, 54.
  ,, legends of creation of, 23, 26, 48-50, 52.
  ,, supposed birthplace of, 38, 53, 260.
Man's happy state, legends of, 44-47, 71.
  ,, development, 249.
Mantras or hymns, 264.
Manu, Laws or Institutes of, 24, 78, 264, 266.
Mars, surface of the planet, 41.
Maruts, Vedic storm-gods, 139, 141.
Mazdâ, see Ahura-Mazdâ
Mecca, 208, 219, 225.
  ,, origin of, 215.
Medina, grave reserved for Christ at, 213.

Melech, a Semitic god, 202.
Men, early races of, in Europe, 61.
Mencius, 278.
Messiah, the Persian, 164.
Meteors, origin of, 31.
Milky Way, the, 11.
Mitra, Vedic sun-god, 117, 139.
Mohammad, sketch of the life of, 208, etc.
  ,, teaching of, 213-217.
Mohammadanism, see Islám,
Moloch, a Semitic god, 202.
Mongol race, 65, 134, 182.
Mongolian legend of the first men, 45.
Monks, Buddhist, 187, 188.
Moon believed to be alive, 87.
  ,, Greek notion of size of, 11.
Moon-plant, see Soma.
Moons, cooling of, 34.
  ,, once white-hot, 30.
  ,, origin of, 30.
'Mother,' meaning of, 77.
  ,, earth addressed as, 87.
Muir, Dr, quoted, 265.
Müller, Max, quoted, 89, 105, 145, 167, 271.
'Muslim,' meaning of, 204.
Myth, origin of, 102-106.
  ,, of battle between light and darkness, 106.
  ,, of the dawn, 102, 104.
Myths, Aryan, 96-126.
  ,, Semitic, 126, 256.
  ,, common origin of certain, 98, 106, etc.
  ,, concerning a happy past, 44-47.

N.

Nats, Buddhist abode of, 273.
Nature, personification of, 87, 89.
Nature of man religious, 250.
Nature-myths, 102-104, 113.
  ,, worship, Aryan, 86-89.
Nebulæ, 41.
Nebular theory of origin of solar systems, 29-31, 258.
Nirvâna, 184, 273.
Norseman's idea of death, 27.
Numbers, sacred, 20, 21.
Nurse Gloaming, 105.

O.

Oceans; how formed, 35.

286

INDEX.

Odin as Alfadir (All Father), 26, 215.
  ,, Valfadir (Choosing Father), 27, 244.
Œdipus, myth of, 100.
Old Woman and pig, tale of, 126.
Om, symbol of Hindu Trinity, 152.
Ordeal, trial by, 77
Origin of myth, 102-106, 113.
  ,, sacrifice, 91.
  ,, the solar system, 29-31, 258.
Ormuzd, Persian god of light, 23, 46, 70, 159, 160, etc., 272.
Ouranos, 110.
Oxygen in the earth's crust, 40.

P.

Pali language, the, 275.
Pârsîs, 23, 158, 271.
  ,, belief of, in a future life, 164, 166.
  ,, fire-worshippers, so-called, 165.
  ,, legend of a happy past, 44.
Persia, ancient importance of, 166.
Persian legend of the Creation, 23.
  ,, ,, first man and woman, 46.
Personification of nature, 89.
Pitaka, *see* Tripitaka.
Planets, origin of the, 30.
  ,, cooling of, 34.
  ,, once suns, 34.
Polynesian idea of foreigners, 14.
Prayer, 91.
  ,, to Varuna, a Vedic god, 146, 147.
  ,, Korân on, 216, 228.
Priestcraft, origin of, 92.
Prithivî, Vedic earth-god, 139, 141.
Proctor, R. A., on origin of solar system, 258.
Promêtheus, myth of, 45.
Psychê and Cupid, myth of, 120.
Punchkin, Hindu fairy tale of, 122.
Purânas, 265, 269.

R.

Races, earliest, of men in Europe, 61, 63.
Râma, 267.
Râmâyana, 264, 267.
Religion of ancient Egyptians, 241.
  ,, ,, Greeks, 242.
Religion of ancient Romans, 243.
  ,, ,, Teutons, 244.
  ,, Buddhist, 170, etc.
  ,, Hindu, 136, etc.
  ,, Mohammadan, 204, etc.
  ,, Pârsî, 158, etc.
  ,, Christian, relation of, to other religions, 246-248.
Religions of China, 189, etc.
Resurrection, 164, 223.
Revelation, book-, 139, 230.
Reynard the Fox, 125.
Rhodopê, myth of, 118.
Rig-Veda, 88, 138, 264.
  ,, contents of, 265.
  ,, gods addressed in, 139.
Rishis, Vedic poets, 138.
Rivers; how formed, 35.
Roman Catholicism and Buddhism, likeness between, 187.
Rome, religion of ancient, 243.
Roots of language, 82.

S.

Sabbath, origin of the, 20.
  ,, Mohammadan, 220.
Sacred books of the Brahmans, 138, 264.
  ,, Buddhists, 177, 275.
  ,, Chinese, 195, 277.
  ,, Mohammadans, 225.
  ,, Pârsîs, 159, 271.
  ,, Scandinavians, 26.
  ,, belief in the inspiration of, 231.
Sacred numbers, 20.
  ,, stone of the Kaabah, 208, 211, 214.
Sacred tree of the Buddhists, 174, 183, 274.
Sacrifice, origin of the rite of, 91.
  ,, among the Aryans, 94.
St George and the Dragon, myth of, 106.
Sâkya-Muni (Buddha), 171.
Sâma-Veda, 264, 265.
Sanhitâ or collection, 264.
Sanskrit language, 83.
  ,, Vedic, value of, 101.
  ,, word for 'sin,' 145.
Saranyû, the dawn, 112.
Satan, *see* Devil.
Saturn, moons and rings of, 30.
Savages, nature-myths among, 102.
Scandinavian legend of the Creation, 25.

INDEX.

Scandinavian religion, 26, 244.
,, sacrifice of the horse, 95.
Seas; how formed, 35.
'Semitic,' meaning of, 200.
Semitic languages, 83.
,, nations, 200.
,, mythology, 256.
,, race, gods of the, 201.
Serpent-worship, 47, 150.
Seven, choice of, as a sacred number, 20.
,, legends connected with, 21.
Shoo, Chinese Classics, 196, 278.
Siddârtha (Buddha), 171.
Sigurd and Fafnir, myth of, 106.
Sikhs, 156.
'Sin' in Sanskrit, 145.
'Sister,' meaning of, 77.
Siva, one of the Hindu Trinity, 152.
,, described, 153.
,, worship of, 269.
Slavonic race, 67.
,, language, 84.
'Smriti,' meaning of, 139.
Solar systems, origin of, 29-31, 258.
Soma, offering of the, 94, 96, 143, 149, 164, 265.
,, as a god, 94, 139, 142.
Sosiosh, the Persian Messiah, 164.
'Soul,' meaning of, 49.
Spectroscope, the, 41.
Spirits, worship of departed, 47, 190.
'Sruti,' meaning of, 139.
Stalagmite floors of caverns, formation of, 57.
Stars, matter in the, and suns the same, 41.
Stone, sacred, of the Kaabah, 208, 211, 214.
,, circles, 134.
,, tools and weapons, 53, 56, 58, 249.
Sudras, 151.
Sun, origin of the, 30.
,, cause of globe-shape of, 31.
,, myths of the, 103, 108, 112.
,, regarded as alive, 87.
,, -gods in the Veda, 139.
Surâhs of the Korân, 226, etc.
Sûrya, Vedic sun-god, 139.
Sûtras, 264, 266, 276.
Suttee, 150.

T.

Tantalus, myth of, 100, 111.

Tantras, 264, 269.
Taoism, 191.
Tartarus, 28, 111.
Tatar tribes, 65.
Tell, William, legend of, 98, 114.
Temples, origin of, 92.
,, absence of, among the Aryans, 150.
,, Zoroastrians, 165.
Temptation of Buddha, 174.
Ten Commandments of Buddha, 185.
Tertiary rocks, 54.
Teutonic languages, 84.
,, religion, 244.
Tibetan legend of the first men, 45.
,, monasteries, 188.
Tiu, same as Dyaus, Deus, etc., 88.
Tower of Babel, legend of, 73, 257.
'Tower of Silence,' Pârsî, 166.
Tradition, 139.
Transmigration, 150, 273.
Tree, sacred, of the Buddhists, 174, 183, 274.
Trial by ordeal, 77.
,, of animals and lifeless objects as criminals, 259, 260.
'Trimûrti,' meaning of, 152.
Trinity, Hindu, 139, 152.
Tripitaka, 177, 275.
Tuesday, origin of, 88.
Tylor, Dr E. B., quoted, 259, 261.

U.

Upanishads, 264, 267.
Uranus, 28.
Ushas, goddess of the dawn, 139.
,, hymn to, 143.

V.

Vach, Vedic goddess of speech, 95.
Valfadir (Choosing Father), 27, 244.
Valhalla (Hall of the Chosen), 27, 245.
Varuna, Vedic god, 111, 139, 144.
,, hymns and prayers to, 146 147.
Vasishtha, a Vedic poet, 144.
'Veda,' meaning of, 138.
Vedângas, 266.
Vedas, 13, 83, 88, 95, 101, 109, 111, 117 142, 147, 151, 153, 170, 240 264.
,, gods invoked in, 139.

Vedas, nature and value of, 137, 264.
„ words of, counted, 139.
Vedic religion, the, 148, 150.
Vermin, Pârsî hatred of, 162.
Vishnu, incarnations of, 153, 267.
„ Vedic sun-god, 139.
„ one of the Hindu Trinity, 152.
Vritra, the dragon, 106, 109, 142, 161.

W.

Wars of Mohammad, 222.
Weeks, origin of, 21.
'Wheel of the law,' 175.
Wife, Mohammad's first, 209, 219.
Witches and witchcraft, origin of belief in, 169.
Wolf and seven kids, tale of, 111.
Words common to the Aryan races, list of, 85.
Worship, Buddhist forms of, 187.
„ Pârsî, „ 165
„ of ancestors, 190.

Worship of the serpent, 47, 150.

Y.

Yagur-Veda, 264, 265.
Yama and Yami, the first pair, 147, 148, 156.
Yima, King, 44, 148.
Ymir, the Frost-giant, 26.

Z.

Zarathustra, *see* Zoroaster.
Zemzem, the well, 215.
Zend (so-called) language, 83, 271.
Zend-Avesta, 23, 70, 83, 133, 159, 163.
„ contents of the, 271, 272.
Zeupatêr, same as Jupiter, etc., 89.
Zeus, 45, 101, 111.
„ same as Dyaus, etc., 88.
Zoroaster, 133, 141, 158, 271.
Zoroastrianism, 133, 158-169.